# BECOMING AN
# ASSESSMENT–CAPABLE
# VISIBLE
# LEARNER

## GRADES 6–12 • LEVEL 1

## LEARNER'S NOTEBOOK

# BECOMING AN ASSESSMENT-CAPABLE VISIBLE LEARNER

## GRADES 6–12 • LEVEL 1

### DOUGLAS FISHER • NANCY FREY
### JOHN HATTIE • KAREN T. FLORIES

## LEARNER'S NOTEBOOK

Name: _____

Grade: _____

School: _____

CORWIN
A SAGE Publishing Company

FOR INFORMATION:

Corwin

A SAGE Company

2455 Teller Road

Thousand Oaks, California 91320

(800) 233-9936

www.corwin.com

SAGE Publications Ltd.

1 Oliver's Yard

55 City Road

London, EC1Y 1SP

United Kingdom

SAGE Publications India Pvt. Ltd.

B 1/I 1 Mohan Cooperative Industrial Area

Mathura Road, New Delhi 110 044

India

SAGE Publications Asia-Pacific Pte. Ltd.

3 Church Street

#10-04 Samsung Hub

Singapore 049483

*Director and Publisher, Corwin Classroom*: Lisa Luedeke

*Editorial Development Manager*: Julie Nemer

*Senior Editorial Assistant*: Sharon Wu

*Production Editor*: Laureen Gleason

*Copy Editor*: Sarah J. Duffy

*Typesetter*: Integra

*Proofreader*: Victoria Reed-Castro

*Cover and Interior Designer*: Janet Kiesel

Printed in the United States of America.

ISBN 978-1-5063-8703-1

This book is printed on acid-free paper.

SUSTAINABLE FORESTRY INITIATIVE

Certified Sourcing

www.sfiprogram.org

SFI-01268

SFI label applies to text stock

18 19 20 21 22 10 9 8 7 6 5 4 3 2 1

# Contents

**PART I. INTRODUCTION**     vii

**PART II. LESSONS**     1

Lesson 1.   What Is Learning?     2

Lesson 2.   Becoming an Assessment-Capable Visible Learner     11

Lesson 3.   Setting Mastery Goals     18

Lesson 4.   Learning Intentions and Success Criteria: What? So What? Self-Assess!     27

Lesson 5.   What Does Success Look Like?     33

Lesson 6.   Using Success Criteria to Monitor Your Progress     35

Lesson 7.   Taking on the Challenge of Learning     38

Lesson 8.   Selecting the Right Strategies to Help You Learn     42

Lesson 9.   Learning How to Learn     46

Lesson 10.   Is It Time for Feedback?     48

Lesson 11.   Asking the Right Questions to Get the Feedback You Need     51

Lesson 12.   Seeing Errors as Opportunities to Learn     55

Lesson 13.   Using Self-Questioning to Guide Your Learning     59

Lesson 14.   Peer Teaching with Think-Alouds     62

Lesson 15.   Peer Teaching with Reciprocal Teaching     65

**PART III. TOOLS AND RESOURCES**     67

1.   Conceptions of Learning Survey     68

2.   Assessment-Capable Visible Learner Self-Assessment     77

3.   Student Goal Setting Template     83

4.   Learning Intentions and Success Criteria Self-Assessment     95

5.   Co-constructing Success Criteria Template     104

6.   Self-Assessing Your Progress Using Success Criteria Template     107

7.   Learning Strategies Checklist     113

8.   Study Skills Checklist     119

9.   Is It Time for Feedback? Checklist     122

10.   Feedback Question Cards     129

11.   Reflecting on Errors as Opportunities to Learn Template     141

12.   Using Self-Questioning to Guide Your Learning Template     150

13.   Checklist for Peer Teaching with Think-Alouds     159

14.   Student Sentence Starters for Reciprocal Teaching     165

# PART I
# INTRODUCTION

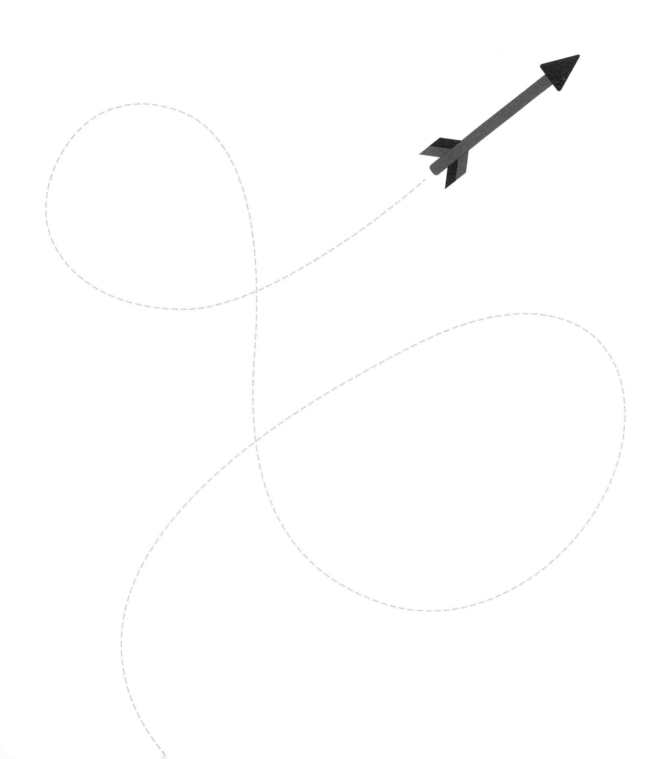

# Introduction

Welcome to the journey of becoming an assessment-capable visible learner! Assessment-capable visible learners have a clear understanding of what they are learning, how they are learning, and where they are going next in their learning. They also understand why they are learning and how it will support them as a learner moving forward. They seek challenges and are open to receiving and giving feedback. Errors are seen as opportunities to learn, and goal setting is an integral part of the learning process. In addition, assessment-capable visible learners can track their progress and monitor their growth so they can define what their next learning steps are. They have the skills and strategies to be their own teacher.

The lessons in this *Learner's Notebook* are designed to help you develop the skills to become an assessment-capable visible learner. The strategies and tools you will learn about and practice in the lessons will help you discover who you are as a learner and equip you with a toolbox of strategies that you can draw from during all of your learning experiences. The strategies can be applied in any of your classes or subjects, so as you progress through them, think about how what you are learning may be a useful tool or strategy to use in another area of your learning. The more you can apply the tools and strategies in all of your learning experiences, the stronger you will become in being an assessment-capable visible learner.

# PART II
## LESSONS

# What Is Learning?

Learning is a complex process. One thing that greatly impacts your learning is the way that you actually think about learning. Today we are going to explore what is called *conceptions of learning*. Conceptions of learning are your ideas and beliefs that you have about being a learner.

Conceptions of learning fall into six categories:

**1** **Learning as gaining information**

**2** **Learning as remembering, using, and understanding information**

**3** **Learning as a duty**

**4** **Learning as personal change**

**5** **Learning as a process not bound by time or place**

**6** **Learning as the development of social competence**

*Think About It*

## A FUN FACT about Conceptions of Learning

Studies show that your conceptions of learning have a direct correlation, or connection, to your academic achievement. So what you think about learning affects your individual success as a learner! It also affects your motivation as a learner and the strategies you select when you are in the learning process.

Let's dig a little deeper into each of the categories by taking the following survey. You'll take this survey multiple times throughout the school year to see if your conceptions of learning change.

## Conceptions of Learning Survey—Time 1

Date: _____

**Directions:** Read each statement carefully and think about how you feel about yourself as a learner. Check the box that best represents your response to each statement. There are no right or wrong answers. The purpose of this survey is to establish a baseline about what *you* think and feel about learning.

| | I think... | Strongly Agree | Agree | Disagree | Strongly Disagree |
|---|---|---|---|---|---|
| 1 | Learning is when I'm taught something that I didn't know before. | | | | |
| 2 | Learning is taking in as many facts as possible. | | | | |
| 3 | When someone gives me new information, I feel like I am learning. | | | | |
| 4 | Learning helps me become clever (quick to understand, learn, apply ideas). | | | | |
| 5 | Learning means I can talk about something in different ways. | | | | |
| 6 | When something stays in my head, I know I have really learned it. | | | | |
| 7 | If I have learned something, it means that I can remember that information whenever I want to. | | | | |
| 8 | I should be able to remember what I have learned at a later date. | | | | |
| 9 | I have really learned something when I can remember it at a later date. | | | | |
| 10 | When I have learned something, I know how to use it in other situations. | | | | |
| 11 | If I know something well, I can use the information if the need arises. | | | | |
| 12 | Learning is making sense out of new information and ways of doing things. | | | | |
| 13 | I know I have learned something when I can explain it to someone else. | | | | |
| 14 | Learning is finding out what things really mean. | | | | |
| 15 | Learning is difficult but important. | | | | |
| 16 | Even when something I am learning is difficult, I must concentrate and keep on trying. | | | | |
| 17 | Learning and studying must be done whether I like it or not. | | | | |
| 18 | Learning has helped me widen my views about life. | | | | |
| 19 | Learning changes my way of thinking. | | | | |
| 20 | By learning, I look at life in new ways. | | | | |

| | I think... | Strongly Agree | Agree | Disagree | Strongly Disagree |
|---|---|---|---|---|---|
| 21 | Learning means I have found new ways to look at things. | | | | |
| 22 | Increased knowledge helps me become a better person. | | | | |
| 23 | I use learning to develop myself as a person. | | | | |
| 24 | When I learn, I think I can change as a person. | | | | |
| 25 | Learning is necessary to help me improve as a person. | | | | |
| 26 | I don't think I will ever stop learning. | | | | |
| 27 | I learn a lot from talking to other people. | | | | |
| 28 | Learning is gaining knowledge through daily experiences. | | | | |
| 29 | Learning is knowing how to get along with different kinds of people. | | | | |
| 30 | Learning is not only studying at school but also knowing how to be considerate to others. | | | | |
| 31 | Learning is the development of common sense in order to become a better member of society. | | | | |
| 32 | Learning is developing good relationships. | | | | |

Count how many check marks you had for each answer choice, and capture the numbers in the table below.

| Strongly Agree | Agree | Disagree | Strongly Disagree |
|---|---|---|---|
| / 32 | / 32 | / 32 | / 32 |

As we continue throughout the school year and work to become assessment-capable visible learners, we will return to this survey tool and see if any of your conceptions of learning have changed.

## Conceptions of Learning Survey—Time 2

Date: _____

**Directions:** Read each statement carefully and think about how you feel about yourself as a learner. Check the box that best represents your response to each statement. There are no right or wrong answers. The purpose of this survey is to establish a baseline about what *you* think and feel about learning.

| | I think... | Strongly Agree | Agree | Disagree | Strongly Disagree |
|---|---|---|---|---|---|
| 1 | Learning is when I'm taught something that I didn't know before. | | | | |
| 2 | Learning is taking in as many facts as possible. | | | | |
| 3 | When someone gives me new information, I feel like I am learning. | | | | |
| 4 | Learning helps me become clever (quick to understand, learn, apply ideas). | | | | |
| 5 | Learning means I can talk about something in different ways. | | | | |
| 6 | When something stays in my head, I know I have really learned it. | | | | |
| 7 | If I have learned something, it means that I can remember that information whenever I want to. | | | | |
| 8 | I should be able to remember what I have learned at a later date. | | | | |
| 9 | I have really learned something when I can remember it at a later date. | | | | |
| 10 | When I have learned something, I know how to use it in other situations. | | | | |
| 11 | If I know something well, I can use the information if the need arises. | | | | |
| 12 | Learning is making sense out of new information and ways of doing things. | | | | |
| 13 | I know I have learned something when I can explain it to someone else. | | | | |
| 14 | Learning is finding out what things really mean. | | | | |
| 15 | Learning is difficult but important. | | | | |
| 16 | Even when something I am learning is difficult, I must concentrate and keep on trying. | | | | |
| 17 | Learning and studying must be done whether I like it or not. | | | | |
| 18 | Learning has helped me widen my views about life. | | | | |
| 19 | Learning changes my way of thinking. | | | | |
| 20 | By learning, I look at life in new ways. | | | | |

| | I think... | Strongly Agree | Agree | Disagree | Strongly Disagree |
|---|---|---|---|---|---|
| 21 | Learning means I have found new ways to look at things. | | | | |
| 22 | Increased knowledge helps me become a better person. | | | | |
| 23 | I use learning to develop myself as a person. | | | | |
| 24 | When I learn, I think I can change as a person. | | | | |
| 25 | Learning is necessary to help me improve as a person. | | | | |
| 26 | I don't think I will ever stop learning. | | | | |
| 27 | I learn a lot from talking to other people. | | | | |
| 28 | Learning is gaining knowledge through daily experiences. | | | | |
| 29 | Learning is knowing how to get along with different kinds of people. | | | | |
| 30 | Learning is not only studying at school but also knowing how to be considerate to others. | | | | |
| 31 | Learning is the development of common sense in order to become a better member of society. | | | | |
| 32 | Learning is developing good relationships. | | | | |

Count how many check marks you had for each answer choice, and capture the numbers in the table below.

| Strongly Agree | Agree | Disagree | Strongly Disagree |
|---|---|---|---|
| / 32 | / 32 | / 32 | / 32 |

Now that you've taken the Conceptions of Learning Survey for the second time this school year, let's look at how these results compare to your results the first time you took the survey.

| Conceptions of Learning Survey **Time 1 Results** | Strongly Agree | Agree | Disagree | Strongly Disagree |
|---|---|---|---|---|
| | / 32 | / 32 | / 32 | / 32 |
| Conceptions of Learning Survey **Time 2 Results** | Strongly Agree | Agree | Disagree | Strongly Disagree |
| | / 32 | / 32 | / 32 | / 32 |
| **Time 1 and Time 2 Changes** | | | | |

**Reflect**

Were there any changes in the way you responded to the statements in the Conceptions of Learning Survey from the first time you took it to the second time? If so, what were they?

What do you think was the cause of those changes?

# Conceptions of Learning Survey—Time 3

Date: _____

**Directions:** Read each statement carefully and think about how you feel about yourself as a learner. Check the box that best represents your response to each statement. There are no right or wrong answers. The purpose of this survey is to establish a baseline about what *you* think and feel about learning.

| | I think... | Strongly Agree | Agree | Disagree | Strongly Disagree |
|---|---|---|---|---|---|
| 1 | Learning is when I'm taught something that I didn't know before. | | | | |
| 2 | Learning is taking in as many facts as possible. | | | | |
| 3 | When someone gives me new information, I feel like I am learning. | | | | |
| 4 | Learning helps me become clever (quick to understand, learn, apply ideas). | | | | |
| 5 | Learning means I can talk about something in different ways. | | | | |
| 6 | When something stays in my head, I know I have really learned it. | | | | |
| 7 | If I have learned something, it means that I can remember that information whenever I want to. | | | | |
| 8 | I should be able to remember what I have learned at a later date. | | | | |
| 9 | I have really learned something when I can remember it at a later date. | | | | |
| 10 | When I have learned something, I know how to use it in other situations. | | | | |
| 11 | If I know something well, I can use the information if the need arises. | | | | |
| 12 | Learning is making sense out of new information and ways of doing things. | | | | |
| 13 | I know I have learned something when I can explain it to someone else. | | | | |
| 14 | Learning is finding out what things really mean. | | | | |
| 15 | Learning is difficult but important. | | | | |
| 16 | Even when something I am learning is difficult, I must concentrate and keep on trying. | | | | |
| 17 | Learning and studying must be done whether I like it or not. | | | | |
| 18 | Learning has helped me widen my views about life. | | | | |
| 19 | Learning changes my way of thinking. | | | | |
| 20 | By learning, I look at life in new ways. | | | | |

| | I think... | Strongly Agree | Agree | Disagree | Strongly Disagree |
|---|---|---|---|---|---|
| 21 | Learning means I have found new ways to look at things. | | | | |
| 22 | Increased knowledge helps me become a better person. | | | | |
| 23 | I use learning to develop myself as a person. | | | | |
| 24 | When I learn, I think I can change as a person. | | | | |
| 25 | Learning is necessary to help me improve as a person. | | | | |
| 26 | I don't think I will ever stop learning. | | | | |
| 27 | I learn a lot from talking to other people. | | | | |
| 28 | Learning is gaining knowledge through daily experiences. | | | | |
| 29 | Learning is knowing how to get along with different kinds of people. | | | | |
| 30 | Learning is not only studying at school but also knowing how to be considerate to others. | | | | |
| 31 | Learning is the development of common sense in order to become a better member of society. | | | | |
| 32 | Learning is developing good relationships. | | | | |

Count how many check marks you had for each answer choice, and capture the numbers in the table below.

| Strongly Agree | Agree | Disagree | Strongly Disagree |
|---|---|---|---|
| / 32 | / 32 | / 32 | / 32 |

Now that you've taken the Conceptions of Learning Survey for the third time this school year, let's look at how these results compare to your results the second time you took the survey.

| Conceptions of Learning Survey **Time 2 Results** | Strongly Agree | Agree | Disagree | Strongly Disagree |
|---|---|---|---|---|
| | / 32 | / 32 | / 32 | / 32 |
| Conceptions of Learning Survey **Time 3 Results** | Strongly Agree | Agree | Disagree | Strongly Disagree |
| | / 32 | / 32 | / 32 | / 32 |
| Time 2 and Time 3 Changes | | | | |

*Reflect*

Were there any changes in the way you responded to the statements in the Conceptions of Learning Survey from the second time you took it to the third time? If so, what were they?

What do you think was the cause of those changes?

# Becoming an Assessment-Capable Visible Learner

One of the major goals of this class is to support your development in becoming an assessment-capable visible learner. Before we begin talking further about this topic, take a moment to think about what that term means to you: assessment-capable visible learner. Capture your definition in the box below.

**Say It In Your Own Words!**

If you had to create your own definition of an assessment-capable visible learner, what would it be?

**Directions:** Find a partner and share your definition of an assessment-capable visible learner. When you are finished, rate your definitions 1, 2, or 3 using the scoring guide below. *There are no good or bad scores. We are using this activity to better determine where we are as a class in having a shared language of learning around the term assessment-capable visible learner.*

## 1
We were almost identical in how we captured the definition of an assessment-capable visible learner, with no more than one difference.

## 2
We had multiple similarities and differences in how we captured the definition of an assessment-capable visible learner.

## 3
Our definitions of an assessment-capable visible learner were very different, with no more than one similarity, if any.

Let's take a look at the list of assessment-capable visible learner characteristics below. Do you see connections to the definitions that you and your partner created?

As an assessment-capable visible learner...

- I know my current level of understanding.
  - I think about what I already know about the learning intention and success criteria.
  - I think about where something will be difficult for me in my learning.
- I know where I am going in my learning.
  - I understand the learning intention and success criteria.
  - I know what I need to do to be successful.
- I look for challenges in my learning.
  - I don't give up when things get hard for me.
  - I look for ways to grow in my learning.
- I can select the right tools to help me when I'm learning.
  - I have different strategies to use when I'm learning.
  - I know what to do when I get stuck in my learning.

- I look for feedback in my learning.
  - I use feedback to help me understand my progress.
  - I ask my classmates for feedback.
  - I ask my teacher for feedback.
- I know mistakes are a good part of my learning.
  - I know that when I make mistakes, it helps me grow.
  - I know when I have to make changes in my learning.
- I know my next steps in learning.
  - I can use the learning intention and success criteria to monitor my progress.
  - I know what I need to do next to grow in my learning.
- I learn from my classmates, and they learn from me.
  - I learn from my classmates during my learning.
  - I teach my classmates when they don't understand something.

**What does being an assessment-capable visible learner *mean* and *look like* in our class?**

| As an assessment-capable visible learner... | What does it mean? | What does it look like in our class? |
| --- | --- | --- |
| I think about what I already know about the learning intention and success criteria. | | |
| I think about where something will be difficult for me in my learning. | | |

| As an assessment-capable visible learner... | What does it mean? | What does it look like in our class? |
| --- | --- | --- |
| I understand the learning intention and success criteria. | | |
| I know what I need to do to be successful. | | |
| I don't give up when things get hard for me. | | |
| I look for ways to grow in my learning. | | |
| I have different strategies to use when I'm learning. | | |
| I know what to do when I get stuck in my learning. | | |
| I use feedback to help me understand my progress. | | |
| I ask my classmates for feedback. | | |

| As an assessment-capable visible learner... | What does it mean? | What does it look like in our class? |
|---|---|---|
| I ask my teacher for feedback. | | |
| I know that when I make mistakes, it helps me grow. | | |
| I know when I have to make changes in my learning. | | |
| I can use the learning intention and success criteria to monitor my progress. | | |
| I know what I need to do next to grow in my learning. | | |
| I learn from my classmates during my learning. | | |
| I teach my classmates when they don't understand something. | | |

Now that we've learned more about what being an assessment-capable visible learner means and looks like in our class, take the self-assessment on the next page. The purpose of the self-assessment is to help identify an area to grow so you can become an assessment-capable visible learner. Nothing is right or wrong, so be honest in your responses.

## Assessment-Capable Visible Learner Self-Assessment

Date: _____

**Directions:** Take a moment to read each statement below, and then check the choice that best represents your response to each statement. Just as with our definitions on page 12, there are no right or wrong choices. You are completing this assessment to determine an action step for yourself as a learner moving forward.

| In this class... | Most of the time | Some of the time | None of the time |
|---|---|---|---|
| I think about what I already know about the learning intention and success criteria. | | | |
| I think about where something will be difficult for me in my learning. | | | |
| I understand the learning intention and success criteria. | | | |
| I know what I need to do to be successful. | | | |
| I don't give up when things get hard for me. | | | |
| I look for ways to grow in my learning. | | | |
| I have different strategies to use when I'm learning. | | | |
| I know what to do when I get stuck in my learning. | | | |
| I use feedback to help me understand my progress. | | | |
| I ask my classmates for feedback. | | | |
| I ask my teacher for feedback. | | | |

| In this class... | Most of the time | Some of the time | None of the time |
|---|---|---|---|
| I know that when I make mistakes, it helps me grow. | | | |
| I know when I have to make changes in my learning. | | | |
| I can use the learning intention and success criteria to monitor my progress. | | | |
| I know what I need to do next to grow in my learning. | | | |
| I learn from my classmates during my learning. | | | |
| I teach my classmates when they don't understand something. | | | |

**Time for Action**

Think about **one** of the areas where you checked "some of the time" or "none of the time." What is an action that you can take to help further develop that area? Capture your action step below.

# Setting Mastery Goals

Goal setting is a critical part of your learning experience, and it is also something that will support you in becoming an assessment-capable visible learner. It is important to set goals, but it is equally important to determine action steps that will support you in meeting your goals and to identify ways in which you will monitor your goals. There are three steps in goal setting:

**1. Identify your goal and understand why it is important.**

**2. Make an action plan and carry it out.**

**3. Reflect on, refine, and, at times, revise your goals.**

 ## Step 1: Identify Your Goal

There are two important components in identifying your goal: *what* your goal is and *why* it is important as your goal. When setting goals, you want to make sure that they are SMARTER. Each letter of SMARTER stands for a piece of criteria that needs to be a part of your goal. These criteria are explained further in the chart below.

| SMARTER Goal | |
|---|---|
| **S · Specific** | Goals need to be specific in what they are going to measure. When writing a goal that is SMARTER, it is important to focus on what it is you want to improve. |
| **M · Measurable** | Goals need to be measurable. There needs to be a way to measure your goal so that you are able to identify whether you have grown from where you originally were to where you are when you meet your goal. |
| **A · Ambitious** | Goals need to be ambitious, which means they need to stretch you as a learner to a new level of learning. The *why* of your goal can help support setting goals that push you to succeed. |
| **R · Results-oriented** | Goals need to be results-oriented. Your goals should focus on an area that will push your performance to the next level. |
| **T · Time bound** | Goals need to be time bound. Dates for completion ensure there is a set time to evaluate progress toward your goal and refine any action steps moving forward. |
| **E · Evaluate** | Goals need to be evaluated. After you establish your goal and begin your plan of action, you need to evaluate your progress toward meeting your goal. This is the time to determine if you need to revise your goal moving forward. |
| **R · Reevaluate** | Goals need to be reevaluated. You don't evaluate your goals only once. Evaluation of your goals in an ongoing process. |

## SMARTER Goal – Student Example

| | |
|---|---|
| **S** · Specific | I will improve my argumentative skills. |
| **M** · Measurable | I will review samples of my argumentative writing using the argumentative writing rubric three times before our final essay is due. I will try to increase by at least one performance level for each section of the rubric. |
| **A** · Ambitious | We have six weeks of instruction that will include lessons that have us practice applying the skills on the argumentative writing rubric. My goal is set so that I will stretch my learning in order to master it. I chose this goal because having strong argumentative skills will help people hear and understand my side of things. |
| **R** · Results-oriented | The goal I have set for myself will push me to grow in my argumentative writing ability. |
| **T** · Time bound | My final argumentative essay is due in eight weeks, on Thursday, March 7. |
| **E** · Evaluate | After I submit my essay, I will know if I met my established goal. If I did, then I will establish a new goal focusing on another skill where I would like to grow. If I don't meet my goal, I will review my action steps to determine what I should continue to do and what I should think about doing differently moving forward. |
| **R** · Reevaluate | I will continue to evaluate the progress I am making toward my current goal. I will also monitor my performance against other targeted skills in this class so that I can keep them connected to my goal setting process. |

# Step 2: Make an Action Plan and Carry It Out

In order to achieve your goal, you need to determine an action plan that will support you. Creating an action plan for your goal can include the following:

- Outlining steps for reaching your goal
- Identifying resources available to support you in reaching your goal
- Specifying ways in which you will monitor and keep track of your progress
- Determining when to evaluate your progress toward meeting your goal

Using the example of the student SMARTER goal on the previous page, let's look at a sample student action plan on the next page.

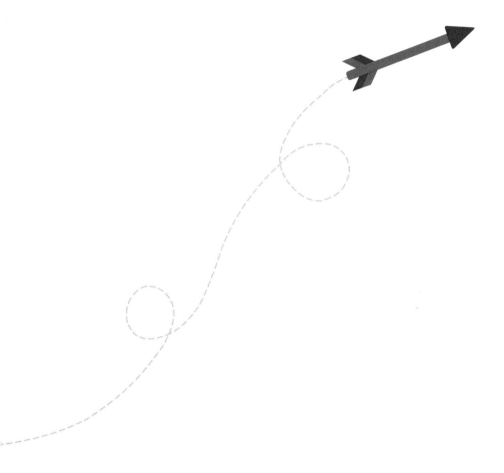

## SMARTER Goal – Student Example

| | |
|---|---|
| **Plan for reaching goal** | 1. Go to the online learning platform outside of class three times a week.<br><br>2. Create a portfolio of tasks in class that focus on the skill in my goal.<br><br>3. Attend tutorial once a week. |
| **Resources available** | 1. Online learning platform<br><br>2. Tutorial sessions with Mrs. Long for close reading and practice tests<br><br>3. Google drive for a place to scan and upload my learning tasks linked to the skill in my goal<br><br>4. Data sheet with preassessment scores |
| **Progress monitoring** | 1. Track and monitor scores on online learning platform for quizzes taken outside of class for growth in skill and increase in Lexile level.<br><br>2. Take practice tests once a week in homeroom tutorial, and track practice test scores.<br><br>3. Review tutorial scores and online learning platform at the end of each week to reflect and make any refinements needed, if any. |
| **Evaluate** | After the unit posttest, I will know if I met my targeted goal. Next steps will be determined based on unit posttest score. It will also help me know where I need to study review. |

# Step 3: Reflect, Refine, and Revise

The third step in the goal setting process occurs after you begin carrying out your action plan for your goal. It is important to stop and reflect upon your goal and then make any adjustments necessary moving forward. Below are some guiding questions that you can use when reflecting, refining, and revising your goal.

1. What actions have I taken so far to support me in meeting my goal?

2. What evidence do I have to determine the impact of those action steps?

3. Does the evidence show growth toward where I want to be?

4. Based on my evidence, do I need to make any adjustments or revisions to my goal?

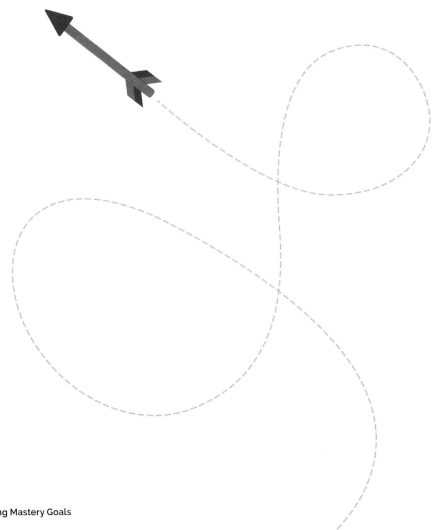

## Student Goal Setting Template

Date: _____

### Step 1: Identify the *what* and *why* of my goal.

What is my goal?

Why is this my goal?

| | Is my goal SMARTER? | |
|---|---|---|
| **S** | **Specific**<br>How is my goal specific? | |
| **M** | **Measurable**<br>How is my goal measurable? | |
| **A** | **Ambitious**<br>How is my goal ambitious? | |
| **R** | **Results-oriented**<br>How is my goal results-oriented? | |
| **T** | **Time bound**<br>How is my goal time bound? | |
| **E** | **Evaluate**<br>How will I evaluate my goal? | |
| **R** | **Reevaluate**<br>How will I reevaluate my plan to reach my goal? | |

## Step 2: Make an action plan and carry it out.

What is my plan for reaching my goal?

What resources do I have available to help me in reaching my goal?

How will I determine my progress toward reaching my goal?

When will I evaluate my goal and determine my next learning steps?

## Step 3: Reflect on, revise, and refine my goal.

What actions have I taken so far to support me in meeting my goal?

What evidence do I have to determine the impact of those action steps?

Does the evidence that I have show growth toward where I want to be?

Based off of my evidence, do I need to make any adjustments or revisions to my goal? If so, what?

# Learning Intentions and Success Criteria: What? So What? Self-Assess!

LESSON

4

**Think About It**

Have you ever been in a class working on an activity but not quite sure why you were working on it or what you were supposed to be learning? Were there ever times when you didn't quite exactly know what you had to do to be successful? There are a lot of students who would answer yes to those questions, which is why we are taking the time to talk about learning intentions and success criteria as a class today, and how you can use them to self-assess yourself as a learner.

## What Are Learning Intentions and Success Criteria?

Learning intentions *describe what you need to learn,* and it is incredibly important that you have a clear understanding of what those learning intentions are. Understanding the learning intentions is a key component of being an assessment-capable visible learner. Learning intentions are created by looking at learning standards for each grade level and subject, and they help define the purpose of the lesson and the skills you need to master. Both you and your teacher should always have a clear picture of your learning destination, and effective learning intentions provide that.

Success criteria represent what you will have to *be able to* do in order to master the learning intention. These are often like steps of a ladder that you will climb. You can use the success criteria to determine whether you are making progress toward the learning intentions.

Let's take a look at a sixth-grade English language arts standard and an example learning intention and success criteria.

---

### 6th-grade ELA standard:

**Cite** textual evidence to **support** the analysis of what the text says explicitly as well as inferences drawn from the text.

---

When we look at the standards for our subject and grade level, we need to look at the *skills and concepts* in the standard. This standard has two major skills that students need to master. Students have to CITE and they have to SUPPORT. See the boldfaced text above in the standard.

Next, we need to think about how students will apply the skill in the standard.

1. With the standard above, what one thing do students need to *cite*?

2. With the standard above, what two things do the students need to *support*?

Now that we've taken a deeper look at what the sixth-grade English language arts standard entails, let's go one step further and think about the learning intentions students will need to master. Here is one example of a learning intention and success criteria for this standard for students who are going to read a story whose main character is a girl named Mary.

| Learning Intention and Success Criteria – Student Example | |
|---|---|
| **Learning Intention:** | I am learning to cite textual evidence to support inferences that I have drawn about a character from the text. |
| **Success Criteria:** | • I can identify key details about Mary's character in the text.<br><br>• I can use the key details to determine three inferences about Mary's character in the text.<br><br>• I can support each inference with two pieces of evidence from the text. |

*Reflect*

How would knowing the learning intention and success criteria for a lesson support you as a learner?

## Why Are Learning Intentions and Success Criteria Important?

What if you found out that tomorrow you were going on a really exciting trip, but you had no idea why you were going there, how you were going to get there, or what you would do once you arrived. It could possibly turn the excitement about the trip into fear because of all of the uncertainty. That can happen in learning, too. Sometimes we don't have a clear destination for what we are learning, why we are learning it, and how we will be successful. That's where learning intentions and success criteria come in. They provide the road map you need as a learner so that you are aware of what you are learning, why you are learning it, and how you will demonstrate success of your learning.

Think about the previous example for the sixth-grade English language arts standard. In looking at the learning intention and success criteria, students have a clear picture of where they need to go in their learning and what they need to do in order to be successful.

Research shows that when you are aware of the learning intentions and success criteria, your learning can grow at double the speed. In order for learning intentions and success criteria to have such an impact on your learning, you need to make sure that you understand what the learning intention and success criteria say. One way to do that is by thinking about what you already know about the learning intention and success criteria for a given lesson.

Let's practice by using the self-assessment on the next page. Your teacher will explain what to write in each of the boxes along the left side of your paper.

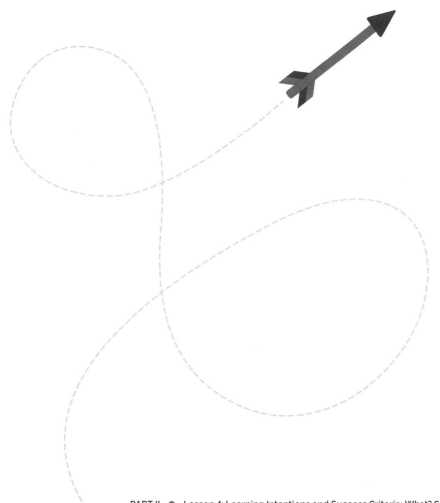

# Learning Intentions and Success Criteria Self-Assessment

Date: _____

| Part 1: What knowledge and experiences do you already have? | | | |
|---|---|---|---|
| **Skills and Concepts** | **I have done this a lot before.** | **I have done this a little before.** | **This will be new for me.** |
| **1** | | | |
| **2** | | | |
| **3** | | | |
| **4** | | | |

## Part 2:

What words or phrases are unclear?

What do I think they might mean?

**Turn & Talk**

Turn to a classmate and share what you captured in your self-assessment and why you checked the choices you did. Next, talk about any words and phrases that might be unclear and what you think they mean.

**Closing Reflection**

A critical part of becoming an assessment-capable visible learner is having a clear understanding of what the learning intentions and success criteria mean. What actions can you take on your own or with your classmates or teacher to ensure you understand the learning intentions of each lesson?

Assessment-capable visible learners know their current level of understanding. In order for you to determine your current level of understanding, you need to know and internalize the learning intentions and success criteria for the lesson. Sometimes, as the teacher, I need support in determining what the success criteria for a lesson are. And what better support than all of you! Today, we are going to co-construct our lesson's success criteria. Which means that as a class we are going to collectively figure out what you would need to show evidence of to prove you have mastered the learning intention.

Before we look at our learning intention(s), let's practice creating success criteria for a different scenario.

| Learning Intention and Success Criteria | |
|---|---|
| **Learning Intention:** | After reading Chapter 6 of *Animal Farm*, describe the contradictions in Napoleon's actions and words. |
| **Success Criteria:** | What would you need to be able to do as evidence that you mastered the learning intention? *Come up with at least three success criteria.* |

## Co-constructing Success Criteria

**Date:** _____

| Today's Learning Intention(s): | |
|---|---|
| Success Criteria: | What would you need to be able to do as evidence that you mastered the learning intention(s)? |

Now that we've taken the time to co-construct success criteria for our learning intention(s), think about the following questions:

1. What will be something that is challenging for you?

2. What will be something you can easily do?

In order to become an assessment-capable visible learner, you need to be able to **self-assess** your learning. Learning intentions and success criteria for a lesson are tools you can use to self-assess. Today, we are going to use a self-assessment tool to help you track your progress using the lesson's success criteria. We will continue to use this tool to self-assess your progress throughout the school year.

## Self-Assessing Your Progress Using Success Criteria

**Date:** _____

**Directions:** Capture the success criteria for the learning intention provided by your teacher in the boxes below. Prior to the end of the lesson, self-assess your progress by determining your performance level for each success criterion below.

| | I'm a pro and can teach others. | I'm able to do this on my own. | I'm still practicing but almost there. | I need more help. |
|---|---|---|---|---|
| **SUCCESS CRITERIA 1:** | | | | |

Evidence to support current performance level:

My next learning steps:

| | | | | |
|---|---|---|---|---|
| **SUCCESS CRITERIA 2:** | | | | |

Evidence to support current performance level:

My next learning steps:

| | I'm a pro and can teach others. | I'm able to do this on my own. | I'm still practicing but almost there. | I need more help. |
|---|---|---|---|---|
| **SUCCESS CRITERIA 3:** | | | | |

Evidence to support current performance level:

My next learning steps:

| | I'm a pro and can teach others. | I'm able to do this on my own. | I'm still practicing but almost there. | I need more help. |
|---|---|---|---|---|
| **SUCCESS CRITERIA 4:** | | | | |

Evidence to support current performance level:

My next learning steps:

## challenge

/'CHalənj/

**noun**

a task or situation that tests someone's abilities.

"the ridge is a challenge for experienced climbers"

synonyms: *problem, difficult task, test, trial*

Challenge is something that should be an integral part of your learning. When learning tasks are challenging, they're usually more fun and worth the effort. In school, there should be opportunities for you to succeed, and there should also be times when you don't initially succeed and need to figure out how to learn from your mistakes in order to grow and move forward. How we see things, especially when we are presented with a challenging or difficult situation, impacts the way in which we will determine how to move forward. Our mindset, or attitude about something, is what will drive how we deal with a challenge. Part of becoming an assessment-capable visible learner requires you to embrace challenges, take risks, and learn from your mistakes. Easier said than done, right?

**Think About It**

Think about a time when you encountered a challenge in your learning. Maybe it was when you were learning something new in math, or completing a lab report in science, or perhaps figuring out how to write your essay in your English class. Whatever the situation was, take a moment to think about how you dealt with that challenge. Did it help you or hurt you in your learning process? Why?

Let's look at a few scenarios. After you read each of the following scenarios, think about how to approach the scenario in a way that would or would not move you forward in your learning.

## Assessment-Capable Visible Learners Seek, Are Resilient, and Aspire to Challenges

Date: _____

### Scenario 1:

You are sitting in math class, and the lesson includes material that you are really struggling with. Not only are you struggling with understanding it, but the teacher also just said that there will be a short quiz on it tomorrow at the end of class. You try to follow along with the steps the teacher is showing the class, but something just isn't making sense for you. You feel your emotions start to build.

How could you look at this challenging situation in a way that *would not* move you forward in your learning?

How could you look at this challenging situation in a way that *would* move you forward in your learning?

### Scenario 2:

The science teacher is asking the class questions about an experiment you just did. You raise your hand to answer one of the questions and get called on to respond. You share your response with the class and it is incorrect. You feel your emotions start to build.

How could you look at this challenging situation in a way that *would not* move you forward in your learning?

How could you look at this challenging situation in a way that *would* move you forward in your learning?

**3**

## Scenario 3:

You just got back an essay you had to write in English class, and you feel like all you see is the red pen with the teacher's comments. You used the rubric as a guide when you were writing your paper, but from the teacher's comments, there were pieces of your essay that didn't fully meet the criteria the teacher set forth. You didn't expect these comments from the teacher. You actually thought you had done well on the essay. You feel your emotions start to build.

How could you look at this challenging situation in a way that *would not* move you forward in your learning?

How could you look at this challenging situation in a way that *would* move you forward in your learning?

# Taking on the Learning Challenge

Date: _____

 **1** What is today's learning challenge?

 **2** How might I feel during the learning challenge? Why?

 **3** What strategies will help me with my learning challenge?

 **4** Did my strategies help me with my learning challenge? Why or why not?

There are many different **strategies** that you can apply to your learning, but knowing what strategy to use and when to use it is critical. When selecting a strategy to support you in your learning, it's important to think about a couple of things. First, you need to know the purpose of your learning. Why are you doing what you are doing? When you know the purpose, it can help you better select appropriate learning strategies. For example, if you know that you are going to be conducting an experiment in your science class, then planning for the task is an effective strategy to select. It is critical for you to be aware of the steps of the experiment, have the supplies and resources that you need, and know the criteria to carry out each step in the experiment. Taking a moment to plan for the task, either individually or with a group of your peers, will help ensure the experiment is carried out safely and effectively.

**Directions:** Take a moment to look through the strategies below. Think about your understanding of each strategy and what it looks like in your learning. Rate each strategy using the following scale:

**1** I fully understand this strategy and know how to apply it in my learning.

**2** I know what this strategy is, but I'm not sure how to use it in my learning.

**3** I have seen or heard of this strategy before, but I'm not sure what it means or how to use it in my learning.

**4** This is a new strategy for me. I don't know what that looks like.

| | | |
|---|---|---|
| _____ Note-taking | _____ Annotating | _____ Self-questioning |
| _____ Outlining | _____ Repeated reading | _____ Self-monitoring |
| _____ Graphic organizers | _____ Summarizing | _____ Planning for the task |
| _____ Concept mapping | _____ Organizing notes | _____ Transforming information |
| _____ Synthesizing information | _____ Deconstructing information | _____ Studying |

Let's look at a couple of other examples of learning experiences and determine a strategy that could help support it.

## Matching Strategies with Learning Tasks

**Directions:** Take a moment to read the description of each sample learning task. Then, in the space provided, write your thoughts about which strategy may be effective and why.

**1**

### Sample Learning Task 1:

The bell just rang for social studies class to begin, and your teacher lets you know that in today's lesson you will be exploring all the different causes and effects of World War I. The teacher is going to give a fifteen-minute lecture providing background information about World War I, and then you will be responsible for reading two different primary sources about the war. There are a lot of details to remember that you will need later in order to determine and support your explanation for the causes and effects of World War I.

What might be an effective strategy to use for this learning task?

Why is it an effective strategy?

**2**

### Sample Learning Task 2:

For the past two days in class you have been learning about all the pieces included in an effective argumentative essay, and now you need to start thinking about the design of your own argumentative essay. You can choose from a few options of texts and topics to use for your essay, so you need to figure out how to get started. Before you turn in a final essay, you'll need to submit a rough draft to your teacher. You'll have class time to work on this, but you'll also need to spend some time on this essay outside of class.

What might be an effective strategy to use for this learning task?

Why is it an effective strategy?

Now that you've taken a look at a couple of sample learning tasks, let's focus on what you are learning today and what strategies can support your learning.

## Learning Strategies Checklist

**Date:** _____

**Directions:** Think about what you are learning today. Check the boxes that most closely reflect your learning task.

## Today your task entails...

| | | |
|---|---|---|
| Writing an essay/paper | Solving problems | ☐ Analyzing ideas, concepts and/or characters |
| Reading an article | Giving a presentation | ☐ Creating a project |
| Studying a novel | Taking an assessment/test/quiz | ☐ Evaluating ideas, concepts and/or characters |
| Conducting an experiment | Learning a new concept or idea | ☐ Writing a lab report |
| Working (collaboratively) in a group | Analyzing data | ☐ Developing a timeline |
| | | ☐ Other |

**Directions:** Look at the list of strategies below. Check at least one strategy that you will use to support you in what you are learning today.

## Learning Strategies

| | | |
|---|---|---|
| Note-taking | Annotating | ☐ Self-questioning |
| Outlining | Repeated reading | ☐ Self-monitoring |
| Graphic organizer | Summarizing | ☐ Planning for the task |
| Concept mapping | Organizing notes | ☐ Transforming information |
| Synthesizing information | Deconstructing information | ☐ Studying |

**Did it Work?**

Take a moment to think about the strategy you used in your learning today. Why did you select this strategy? Do you think that it supported you in your learning? Why or why not?

We are going to focus on three kinds of **study skills**: cognitive, metacognitive, and affective. Being aware of different study skills and how they support your learning is important to becoming an assessment-capable visible learner.

**1**

**COGNITIVE STUDY SKILLS**
focus on the development of *task-related* skills, such as note-taking and summarizing.

**2**

**METACOGNITIVE STUDY SKILLS**
are *self-management* skills, such as planning and monitoring your progress.

**3**

**AFFECTIVE STUDY SKILLS**
focus on *noncognitive* features of learning, such as motivation, agency, and self-concept.

Think about the different study skills captured in the boxes below. How would these be helpful in our class? Let's think about what you will be focusing on in class and determine how these study skills might best support you in your learning. We will revisit these strategies often so that you can strengthen your ability to choose the right study skills to move you forward in your learning. Eventually, using these strategies will become something that you do without even thinking about it! You should use study skills from each column throughout your learning journey in this class.

| Cognitive Study Skills | Metacognitive Study Skills | Affective Study Skills |
|---|---|---|
| • I can take notes. | • I can plan for my task. | • I can get motivated to study or practice. |
| • I can use a graphic organizer. | • I can monitor my learning. | • I can structure my learning environment. |
| • I can summarize. | • I can review corrected work. | • I can manage my time. |
| • I can create flashcards. | • I can revise my work. | • I can manage my stress and anxiety. |
| • I can use mnemonics. | • I can self-assess. | • I can set goals. |
| • I can memorize important information. | • I can use self-questioning. | • I have a willingness to solve problems. |
| • I can reread. | • I can self-verbalize. | • I desire to influence my own learning. |

# Study Skills Checklist

Date: _____

| Our learning intention: | |
|---|---|
| I need practice with: | |

Check the study skills below that you will use as part of your practice moving forward.

| Cognitive Study Skills | Metacognitive Study Skills | Affective Study Skills |
|---|---|---|
| I can take notes. | I can plan for my task. | ☐ I can get motivated to study or practice. |
| I can use a graphic organizer. | I can monitor my learning. | ☐ I can structure my learning environment. |
| I can summarize. | I can review corrected work. | ☐ I can manage my time. |
| I can create flashcards. | I can revise my work. | ☐ I can manage my stress and anxiety. |
| I can use mnemonics. | I can self-assess. | ☐ I can set goals. |
| I can memorize important information. | I can use self-questioning. | ☐ I have a willingness to solve problems. |
| I can reread. | I can self-verbalize. | ☐ I desire to influence my own learning. |

# Is It Time for Feedback?

**Feedback** plays a major role in your learning. Feedback is kind of like advice you receive to let you know how you are doing and what your next steps might be while you're learning. Part of becoming an assessment-capable visible learner means that not only are you able to receive feedback, but you are also able to determine *when* you need feedback and how you will go about getting it.

Sometimes you can give yourself the feedback that you need to move forward, and other times you may require the support of a peer or the teacher. Feedback's major purpose is to help close the gap from where you are now in your learning to where you need to be. It's incredibly important that you are able to recognize when you need feedback and how to best use feedback.

On the next few pages, there are a few checklists you can use to guide you in seeking feedback, depending on where you are in your learning.

# Is It Time for Feedback? Checklist

Date:_____

| I Can't Get Started in My Learning | |
|---|---|
| What can I do on my own? | ☐ I reread the directions to make sure I didn't miss something.<br>☐ I reviewed the success criteria.<br>☐ I reviewed any examples and/or resources provided for my task.<br>☐ I looked online for examples of others' work. |
| What can I do with a peer? | ☐ I asked my peer to clarify the task.<br>☐ I asked my peer to walk me through the question and/or problem.<br>☐ I asked my peer how they knew how to get started.<br>☐ I asked my peer to support me in getting the task started. |
| What can I do with the teacher? | ☐ I clarified what the task is asking for.<br>☐ I walked through an example/exemplar with the teacher.<br>☐ I asked the teacher to support me in getting the task started. |

| I Got Started, but I'm Not Sure Where to Go Next in My Learning | |
|---|---|
| What can I do on my own? | ☐ I reviewed the success criteria.<br>☐ I reviewed any examples and/or resources provided for my task.<br>☐ I tried to determine where I need to go next based off of what I got started.<br>☐ I determined what I got right so far and why. |
| What can I do with a peer? | ☐ I clarified what the task was asking for.<br>☐ I showed my work to my peer and asked for help in identifying my next step.<br>☐ I asked my peer to ask me questions about what I got started on my task.<br>☐ I asked my peer what they felt I had gotten right so far and why. |
| What can I do with the teacher? | ☐ I clarified what the task is asking for.<br>☐ I asked for support in identifying my next step.<br>☐ I asked the teacher to model the portion of the task I misunderstand. |

| I'm Finished with My Learning | |
|---|---|
| **What can I do on my own?** | I self-assessed my work against the success criteria.<br><br>I reviewed my work against the exemplar, if applicable.<br><br>I identified where I have strengths in my work to get even stronger.<br><br>I identified opportunities in my work to determine what my next learning step is. |
| **What can I do with a peer?** | I asked my peer if they agree that I met the success criteria.<br><br>I asked my peer to identify a strength in my work.<br><br>I asked my peer to identify an opportunity in my work. |
| **What can I do with the teacher?** | I asked my teacher if they agree that I met the success criteria.<br><br>I asked the teacher to identify a strength in my current work.<br><br>I asked the teacher to identify an opportunity in my current work. |

Feedback plays an enormous role in your learning, and seeking feedback is part of becoming an assessment-capable visible learner. Feedback can come from a variety of sources and in different ways. Feedback is much more than just going to the teacher for help. You can give yourself feedback through self-assessment or self-questioning, and you can also lean on your peers and teacher for feedback.

As a learner in this class, it is important not only that you seek feedback, but also that you are able to ask specifically for the type feedback you need. Today, we are going to practice asking for specific feedback by using Feedback Question Cards. The cards have two parts. First, there are questions to help you think about the feedback that you need. You don't necessarily have to write out an answer for each question, as much as you need to read and think about each one. Next, you generate a question to ask a peer or the teacher that is focused on the feedback that you are seeking.

Take a moment to review the Feedback Question Card below. This is one of the tools we will use in class throughout the year to support you in asking specific questions about feedback you need.

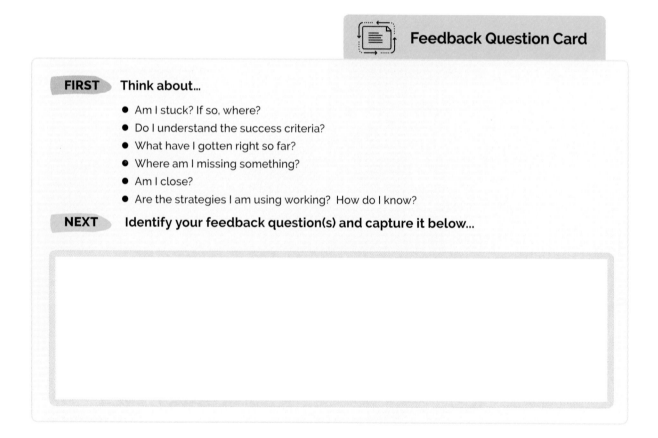

**Feedback Question Card**

**FIRST** **Think about...**

- Am I stuck? If so, where?
- Do I understand the success criteria?
- What have I gotten right so far?
- Where am I missing something?
- Am I close?
- Are the strategies I am using working? How do I know?

**NEXT** **Identify your feedback question(s) and capture it below...**

Before we get started on our own, let's look at a student example of a Feedback Question Card. The student's thinking is in *italics* and her question is in **bold**. Notice how specific the question is that the student created to ask a peer or the teacher. Instead of simply asking for help, the student's question is focused exactly on the information she needs so she can move forward in her learning.

**Feedback Question Card**

**FIRST** Think about…

- **Am I stuck? If so, where?**

  *I don't know how to get the body paragraphs started for my argumentative essay.*

- **Do I understand the success criteria?**

  *I understand the rubric for the essay, I just don't know if my claims, counterclaims, and evidence belong in a certain order.*

- **What have I gotten right so far?**

  *I know that I wrote my introductory paragraph correctly for my argumentative essay because we had to submit our draft for approval.*

- **Where am I missing something?**

- **Am I close?**

- **Are the strategies I am using working? How do I know?**

  *I'm looking at the outline I made for my essay, but I'm still not sure how to structure my body paragraphs. I also reviewed the rubric, so I know I have what needs to go in the body paragraphs, but I'm still confused on the structure.*

**NEXT** Identify your feedback question(s) and capture it below…

Is there a specific structure that I need to use to have my claims, counterclaims, and evidence appear in each of my body paragraphs for my argumentative essay?

Now let's try it out on our own with what we will be learning about today.

**Feedback Question Card**

**FIRST** Think about...

- Am I stuck? If so, where?
- Do I understand the success criteria?
- What have I gotten right so far?
- Where am I missing something?
- Am I close?
- Are the strategies I am using working? How do I know?

**NEXT** Identify your feedback question(s) and capture it below...

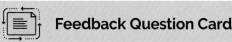 **Feedback Question Card**

**FIRST** Think about...

- Am I stuck? If so, where?
- Do I understand the success criteria?
- What have I gotten right so far?
- Where am I missing something?
- Am I close?
- Are the strategies I am using working? How do I know?

**NEXT** Identify your feedback question(s) and capture it below...

**Feedback Question Card**

**FIRST** Think about...

- Am I stuck? If so, where?
- Do I understand the success criteria?
- What have I gotten right so far?
- Where am I missing something?
- Am I close?
- Are the strategies I am using working? How do I know?

**NEXT** Identify your feedback question(s) and capture it below...

 **Feedback Question Card**

**FIRST** Think about...

- Am I stuck? If so, where?
- Do I understand the success criteria?
- What have I gotten right so far?
- Where am I missing something?
- Am I close?
- Are the strategies I am using working? How do I know?

**NEXT** Identify your feedback question(s) and capture it below...

**Think About It**

Stop and think about a time when you made a mistake or an error. It doesn't have to be an example connected to school; it can be anything. You could have been drawing, singing, playing a sport, cooking, talking, skateboarding. Any experience will work that you can think of when you made an error. How did you feel about it? Why did you feel that way? How did you move forward?

Becoming an assessment-capable visible learner means that you can look at the **errors** you make in your learning as opportunities to grow and build on. Today you are going to look at recent assessment results and use the chart on the next page to self-assess your performance. You will then use your errors to identify areas for growth moving forward.

## Reflecting on Errors as Opportunities to Learn

Date: _____

**Directions:** Read and review the questions on your assessment. As you go through each one, place the question number in one of the four quadrants below.

Questions that I thought were
**EASY** that I got **WRONG**

Questions that I thought were
**HARD** that I got **WRONG**

Questions that I thought were
**EASY** that I got **RIGHT**

Questions that I thought were
**HARD** that I got **RIGHT**

## Questions that I thought were **EASY** that I got **WRONG**

**Question #:**

Why did you get it wrong?

What do you need to learn to get it right next time?

**Question #:**

Why did you get it wrong?

What do you need to learn to get it right next time?

**Question #:**

Why did you get it wrong?

What do you need to learn to get it right next time?

**Question #:**

Why did you get it wrong?

What do you need to learn to get it right next time?

## Questions that I thought were **HARD** that I got **WRONG**

**Question #:**

What about the question was hard for you?

What do you need to learn to get it right next time?

**Question #:**

What about the question was hard for you?

What do you need to learn to get it right next time?

**Question #:**

What about the question was hard for you?

What do you need to learn to get it right next time?

**Question #:**

What about the question was hard for you?

What do you need to learn to get it right next time?

## Using Self-Questioning to Guide Your Learning

**Date:** _____

Self-questioning is when you generate questions to ask yourself during different phases of your learning. Asking yourself questions *before, during*, and *after* you engage in learning tasks is a strategy you can use to help yourself develop as an assessment-capable visible learner. Today, we will practice applying self-questioning to the lesson we are going to focus on.

### BEFORE THE LESSON...

What am I learning today?  What is the learning intention?

What do I already know about this?

What do I want to know about this?

What do I need to do or find out?

**DURING THE LESSON...**

What am I finding out?

What questions do I have as I'm learning?

What is confusing to me?

What do I still need to find out?

## AFTER THE LESSON...

What did I learn as a result of the lesson?

What is still confusing or challenging for me?

What do I still need to do moving forward?

# LESSON 14

## Peer Teaching with Think-Alouds

Today, you are going to help teach your peers through a strategy called a **think-aloud**. The purpose of a think-aloud is to voice the internal cognitive and metacognitive decisions you are making during the act of reading a passage. Basically, you invite someone into your mind and share with them what you are thinking, why you are thinking it, and what action it's causing you to take. Your teacher will model a think-aloud process before you engage in one with your peers. There is also a checklist on the next page to support you in your think-aloud.

## Checklist for Peer Teaching with Think-Alouds

**Date:** _____

### Thinking during a Think-Aloud Checklist

Let everyone who will be listening to your think-aloud read through the question or text before you begin your think-aloud.

Use "I" statements.

Share what you are reading about.

Talk about what is catching your attention as a reader.

Explain why you think you are correct using evidence in the text.

Don't go too fast or too slow.

Determine any actions you are taking as a result of what you are thinking about as you read.

Share why you are taking the actions you are taking.

Make sure your think-aloud isn't longer than five minutes.

**Stop & Reflect**

1. What was it like *doing* a think-aloud for your peer(s)? Did it support you in what you were learning today? Why or why not?

2. What was it like *listening* to a think-aloud from your peer(s)? Did it support you in what you were learning today? Why or why not?

**Reciprocal Teaching:** When students read collaboratively in small groups using text that has been segmented into passages of a few paragraphs each. At each stopping point, the group has a discussion about what they have just read using four comprehension strategies:

**1** **Summarizing:** capturing the key messages and understandings of what was read

**2** **Questioning:** asking questions about what was just read to help better understand the text

**3** **Clarifying:** identifying where there are words or ideas that are confusing in what was just read

**4** **Predicting:** thinking about what was read and taking a guess about what might happen next

Part of becoming an assessment-capable visible learner is positively supporting your peers', or fellow classmates', learning. Engaging in reciprocal teaching is one strategy that you can use to do that. As we read today, your group is going to use reciprocal teaching. On the next page are some sentence starters to use to help you get started with each strategy.

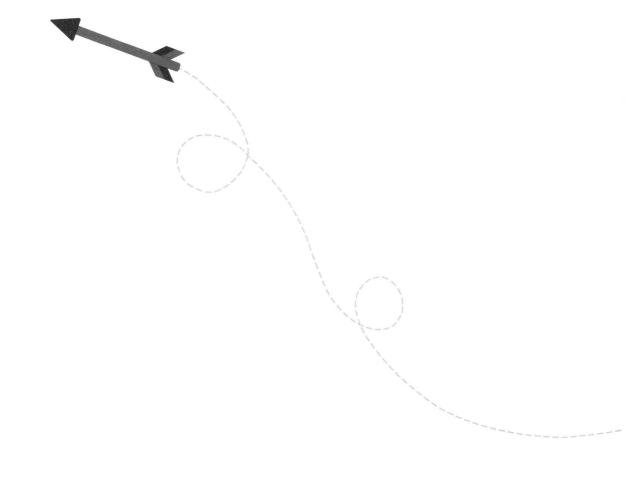

# Student Sentence Starters for Reciprocal Teaching

Date: _____

| | |
|---|---|
| **Summarizing** | • *Key details in this passage are...* <br><br> • *Key information included in this passage is...* <br><br> • *The main idea/message of the passage is...* <br><br> • *A theme I can see is...* <br><br> • *A summary of what we just read is...* |
| **Questioning** | • *What does the passage mean where it said...?* <br><br> • *Why did the author choose to include...?* (This could be key vocabulary, pictures, symbols, graphs, etc.) <br><br> • *What is the point of...?* <br><br> • *Why is ... happening?* <br><br> • *What is the relationship between...?* (This could be relationships between characters, ideas, concepts, numbers, places, etc.) <br><br> • *What can we infer about...?* (This could be relationships between characters, ideas, concepts, numbers, places, etc.) <br><br> • *What evidence in the text supports...?* |
| **Clarifying** | • *Is the author saying... about...?* <br><br> • *What does this word or phrase mean?* (Share the word or phrase with the group.) <br><br> • *Can you elaborate on what you just said about...?* <br><br> • *Tell me more about...?* <br><br> • *What evidence supports what you just shared?* <br><br> • *Can you give me an example of...?* |
| **Predicting** | • *I think the next passage we read is going to be about...* <br><br> • *Information that will probably be a part of the next passage is...* <br><br> • *I bet we'll learn more about...in the next passage.* <br><br> • *I think we'll find out about...in the next passage.* |

# PART III
# TOOLS AND RESOURCES

1. Conceptions of Learning Survey 68
2. Assessment-Capable Visible Learner Self-Assessment 77
3. Student Goal Setting Template 83
4. Learning Intentions and Success Criteria Self-Assessment 95
5. Co-constructing Success Criteria Template 104
6. Self-Assessing Your Progress Using Success Criteria Template 107
7. Learning Strategies Checklist 113
8. Study Skills Checklist 119
9. Is It Time for Feedback? Checklist 122
10. Feedback Question Cards 129
11. Reflecting on Errors as Opportunities to Learn Template 141
12. Using Self-Questioning to Guide Your Learning Template 150
13. Checklist for Peer Teaching with Think-Alouds 159
14. Student Sentence Starters for Reciprocal Teaching 165

# Conceptions of Learning Survey

**Date:** _____

**Directions:** Read each statement carefully and think about how you feel about yourself as a learner. Check the box that best represents your response to each statement. There are no right or wrong answers. The purpose of this survey is to establish a baseline about what *you* think and feel about learning.

| | *I think...* | Strongly Agree | Agree | Disagree | Strongly Disagree |
|---|---|---|---|---|---|
| 1 | Learning is when I'm taught something that I didn't know before. | | | | |
| 2 | Learning is taking in as many facts as possible. | | | | |
| 3 | When someone gives me new information, I feel like I am learning. | | | | |
| 4 | Learning helps me become clever (quick to understand, learn, apply ideas). | | | | |
| 5 | Learning means I can talk about something in different ways. | | | | |
| 6 | When something stays in my head, I know I have really learned it. | | | | |
| 7 | If I have learned something, it means that I can remember that information whenever I want to. | | | | |
| 8 | I should be able to remember what I have learned at a later date. | | | | |
| 9 | I have really learned something when I can remember it at a later date. | | | | |
| 10 | When I have learned something, I know how to use it in other situations. | | | | |
| 11 | If I know something well, I can use the information if the need arises. | | | | |
| 12 | Learning is making sense out of new information and ways of doing things. | | | | |
| 13 | I know I have learned something when I can explain it to someone else. | | | | |
| 14 | Learning is finding out what things really mean. | | | | |
| 15 | Learning is difficult but important. | | | | |
| 16 | Even when something I am learning is difficult, I must concentrate and keep on trying. | | | | |
| 17 | Learning and studying must be done whether I like it or not. | | | | |
| 18 | Learning has helped me to widen my views about life. | | | | |
| 19 | Learning changes my way of thinking. | | | | |
| 20 | By learning, I look at life in new ways. | | | | |

| | I think... | Strongly Agree | Agree | Disagree | Strongly Disagree |
|---|---|---|---|---|---|
| 21 | Learning means I have found new ways to look at things. | | | | |
| 22 | Increased knowledge helps me become a better person. | | | | |
| 23 | I use learning to develop myself as a person. | | | | |
| 24 | When I learn, I think I can change as a person. | | | | |
| 25 | Learning is necessary to help me improve as a person. | | | | |
| 26 | I don't think that I will ever stop learning. | | | | |
| 27 | I learn a lot from talking to other people. | | | | |
| 28 | Learning is gaining knowledge through daily experiences. | | | | |
| 29 | Learning is knowing how to get along with different kinds of people. | | | | |
| 30 | Learning is not only studying at school but also knowing how to be considerate to others. | | | | |
| 31 | Learning is the development of common sense in order to become a better member of society. | | | | |
| 32 | Learning is developing good relationships. | | | | |

Count how many check marks you had for each answer choice, and capture the numbers in the table below.

| Strongly Agree | Agree | Disagree | Strongly Disagree |
|---|---|---|---|
| _____ / 32 | _____ / 32 | _____ / 32 | _____ / 32 |

Now that you've taken the Conceptions of Learning Survey, let's look at how these results compare to your previous results.

| Conceptions of Learning Survey Time _____ Results | Strongly Agree | Agree | Disagree | Strongly Disagree |
|---|---|---|---|---|
| | _____ / 32 | _____ / 32 | _____ / 32 | _____ / 32 |
| Conceptions of Learning Survey Time _____ Results | Strongly Agree | Agree | Disagree | Strongly Disagree |
| | _____ / 32 | _____ / 32 | _____ / 32 | _____ / 32 |
| Time _____ and Time _____ Changes | | | | |

**Reflect**

Were there any changes in the way you responded to the statements in the Conceptions of Learning Survey from the last time you took it to this time? If so, what were they?

What do you think was the cause of those changes?

# Conceptions of Learning Survey

Date: _____

**Directions:** Read each statement carefully and think about how you feel about yourself as a learner. Check the box that best represents your response to each statement. There are no right or wrong answers. The purpose of this survey is to establish a baseline about what *you* think and feel about learning.

| | I think... | Strongly Agree | Agree | Disagree | Strongly Disagree |
|---|---|---|---|---|---|
| 1 | Learning is when I'm taught something that I didn't know before. | | | | |
| 2 | Learning is taking in as many facts as possible. | | | | |
| 3 | When someone gives me new information, I feel like I am learning. | | | | |
| 4 | Learning helps me become clever (quick to understand, learn, apply ideas). | | | | |
| 5 | Learning means I can talk about something in different ways. | | | | |
| 6 | When something stays in my head, I know I have really learned it. | | | | |
| 7 | If I have learned something, it means that I can remember that information whenever I want to. | | | | |
| 8 | I should be able to remember what I have learned at a later date. | | | | |
| 9 | I have really learned something when I can remember it at a later date. | | | | |
| 10 | When I have learned something, I know how to use it in other situations. | | | | |
| 11 | If I know something well, I can use the information if the need arises. | | | | |
| 12 | Learning is making sense out of new information and ways of doing things. | | | | |
| 13 | I know I have learned something when I can explain it to someone else. | | | | |
| 14 | Learning is finding out what things really mean. | | | | |
| 15 | Learning is difficult but important. | | | | |
| 16 | Even when something I am learning is difficult, I must concentrate and keep on trying. | | | | |
| 17 | Learning and studying must be done whether I like it or not. | | | | |
| 18 | Learning has helped me to widen my views about life. | | | | |
| 19 | Learning changes my way of thinking. | | | | |
| 20 | By learning, I look at life in new ways. | | | | |

| | I think... | Strongly Agree | Agree | Disagree | Strongly Disagree |
|---|---|---|---|---|---|
| 21 | Learning means I have found new ways to look at things. | | | | |
| 22 | Increased knowledge helps me become a better person. | | | | |
| 23 | I use learning to develop myself as a person. | | | | |
| 24 | When I learn, I think I can change as a person. | | | | |
| 25 | Learning is necessary to help me improve as a person. | | | | |
| 26 | I don't think that I will ever stop learning. | | | | |
| 27 | I learn a lot from talking to other people. | | | | |
| 28 | Learning is gaining knowledge through daily experiences. | | | | |
| 29 | Learning is knowing how to get along with different kinds of people. | | | | |
| 30 | Learning is not only studying at school but also knowing how to be considerate to others. | | | | |
| 31 | Learning is the development of common sense in order to become a better member of society. | | | | |
| 32 | Learning is developing good relationships. | | | | |

Count how many check marks you had for each answer choice, and capture the numbers in the table below.

| Strongly Agree | Agree | Disagree | Strongly Disagree |
|---|---|---|---|
| _____ / 32 | _____ / 32 | _____ / 32 | _____ / 32 |

Now that you've taken the Conceptions of Learning Survey, let's look at how these results compare to your previous results.

| Conceptions of Learning Survey Time _____ Results | Strongly Agree | Agree | Disagree | Strongly Disagree |
|---|---|---|---|---|
| | _____ / 32 | _____ / 32 | _____ / 32 | _____ / 32 |
| Conceptions of Learning Survey Time _____ Results | Strongly Agree | Agree | Disagree | Strongly Disagree |
| | _____ / 32 | _____ / 32 | _____ / 32 | _____ / 32 |
| Time _____ and Time _____ Changes | | | | |

**Reflect**

Were there any changes in the way you responded to the statements in the Conceptions of Learning Survey from the last time you took it to this time? If so, what were they?

What do you think was the cause of those changes?

# Conceptions of Learning Survey

Date: _____

**Directions:** Read each statement carefully and think about how you feel about yourself as a learner. Check the box that best represents your response to each statement. There are no right or wrong answers. The purpose of this survey is to establish a baseline about what *you* think and feel about learning.

| | *I think...* | Strongly Agree | Agree | Disagree | Strongly Disagree |
|---|---|---|---|---|---|
| 1 | Learning is when I'm taught something that I didn't know before. | | | | |
| 2 | Learning is taking in as many facts as possible. | | | | |
| 3 | When someone gives me new information, I feel like I am learning. | | | | |
| 4 | Learning helps me become clever (quick to understand, learn, apply ideas). | | | | |
| 5 | Learning means I can talk about something in different ways. | | | | |
| 6 | When something stays in my head, I know I have really learned it. | | | | |
| 7 | If I have learned something, it means that I can remember that information whenever I want to. | | | | |
| 8 | I should be able to remember what I have learned at a later date. | | | | |
| 9 | I have really learned something when I can remember it at a later date. | | | | |
| 10 | When I have learned something, I know how to use it in other situations. | | | | |
| 11 | If I know something well, I can use the information if the need arises. | | | | |
| 12 | Learning is making sense out of new information and ways of doing things. | | | | |
| 13 | I know I have learned something when I can explain it to someone else. | | | | |
| 14 | Learning is finding out what things really mean. | | | | |
| 15 | Learning is difficult but important. | | | | |
| 16 | Even when something I am learning is difficult, I must concentrate and keep on trying. | | | | |
| 17 | Learning and studying must be done whether I like it or not. | | | | |
| 18 | Learning has helped me to widen my views about life. | | | | |
| 19 | Learning changes my way of thinking. | | | | |
| 20 | By learning, I look at life in new ways. | | | | |

| | I think... | Strongly Agree | Agree | Disagree | Strongly Disagree |
|---|---|---|---|---|---|
| 21 | Learning means I have found new ways to look at things. | | | | |
| 22 | Increased knowledge helps me become a better person. | | | | |
| 23 | I use learning to develop myself as a person. | | | | |
| 24 | When I learn, I think I can change as a person. | | | | |
| 25 | Learning is necessary to help me improve as a person. | | | | |
| 26 | I don't think that I will ever stop learning. | | | | |
| 27 | I learn a lot from talking to other people. | | | | |
| 28 | Learning is gaining knowledge through daily experiences. | | | | |
| 29 | Learning is knowing how to get along with different kinds of people. | | | | |
| 30 | Learning is not only studying at school but also knowing how to be considerate to others. | | | | |
| 31 | Learning is the development of common sense in order to become a better member of society. | | | | |
| 32 | Learning is developing good relationships. | | | | |

Count how many check marks you had for each answer choice, and capture the numbers in the table below.

| Strongly Agree | Agree | Disagree | Strongly Disagree |
|---|---|---|---|
| _____ / 32 | _____ / 32 | _____ / 32 | _____ / 32 |

Now that you've taken the Conceptions of Learning Survey, let's look at how these results compare to your previous results.

| Conceptions of Learning Survey Time ____ Results | Strongly Agree | Agree | Disagree | Strongly Disagree |
|---|---|---|---|---|
| | _____ / 32 | _____ / 32 | _____ / 32 | _____ / 32 |
| Conceptions of Learning Survey Time ____ Results | Strongly Agree | Agree | Disagree | Strongly Disagree |
| | _____ / 32 | _____ / 32 | _____ / 32 | _____ / 32 |
| Time _____ and Time _____ Changes | | | | |

**Reflect**

Were there any changes in the way you responded to the statements in the Conceptions of Learning Survey from the last time you took it to this time? If so, what were they?

What do you think was the cause of those changes?

# Assessment-Capable Visible Learner Self-Assessment

Date: _____

**Directions:** Take a moment to complete the assessment-capable visible learner self-assessment below. Read each statement and then check the choice that best represents your response to each statement. There are no right or wrong choices. You are completing this assessment to determine an action step for yourself as a learner moving forward.

| In this class... | Most of the time | Some of the time | None of the time |
|---|---|---|---|
| I think about what I already know about the learning intention and success criteria. | | | |
| I think about where something will be difficult for me in my learning. | | | |
| I understand the learning intention and success criteria. | | | |
| I know what I need to do to be successful. | | | |
| I don't give up when things get hard for me. | | | |
| I look for ways to grow in my learning. | | | |
| I have different strategies to use when I'm learning. | | | |
| I know what to do when I get stuck in my learning. | | | |
| I use feedback to help me understand my progress. | | | |
| I ask my classmates for feedback. | | | |
| I ask my teacher for feedback. | | | |
| I know that when I make mistakes, it helps me grow. | | | |
| I know when I have to make changes in my learning. | | | |
| I can use the learning intention and success criteria to monitor my progress. | | | |
| I know what I need to do next to grow in my learning. | | | |
| I learn from my classmates during my learning. | | | |
| I teach my classmates when they don't understand something. | | | |

Think about **one** of the areas where you checked "some of the time" or "none of the time." What is an action you can take to help further develop that area? Capture your action step below.

# Assessment-Capable Visible Learner Self-Assessment

**Date:** _____

**Directions:** Take a moment to complete the assessment-capable visible learner self-assessment below. Read each statement and then check the choice that best represents your response to each statement. There are no right or wrong choices. You are completing this assessment to determine an action step for yourself as a learner moving forward.

| In this class... | Most of the time | Some of the time | None of the time |
| --- | --- | --- | --- |
| I think about what I already know about the learning intention and success criteria. | | | |
| I think about where something will be difficult for me in my learning. | | | |
| I understand the learning intention and success criteria. | | | |
| I know what I need to do to be successful. | | | |
| I don't give up when things get hard for me. | | | |
| I look for ways to grow in my learning. | | | |
| I have different strategies to use when I'm learning. | | | |
| I know what to do when I get stuck in my learning. | | | |
| I use feedback to help me understand my progress. | | | |
| I ask my classmates for feedback. | | | |
| I ask my teacher for feedback. | | | |
| I know that when I make mistakes, it helps me grow. | | | |
| I know when I have to make changes in my learning. | | | |
| I can use the learning intention and success criteria to monitor my progress. | | | |
| I know what I need to do next to grow in my learning. | | | |
| I learn from my classmates during my learning. | | | |
| I teach my classmates when they don't understand something. | | | |

**Time for Action**

Think about **one** of the areas where you checked "some of the time" or "none of the time." What is an action you can take to help further develop that area? Capture your action step below.

# Assessment-Capable Visible Learner Self-Assessment

Date: _____

**Directions:** Take a moment to complete the assessment-capable visible learner self-assessment below. Read each statement and then check the choice that best represents your response to each statement. There are no right or wrong choices. You are completing this assessment to determine an action step for yourself as a learner moving forward.

| In this class... | Most of the time | Some of the time | None of the time |
|---|---|---|---|
| I think about what I already know about the learning intention and success criteria. | | | |
| I think about where something will be difficult for me in my learning. | | | |
| I understand the learning intention and success criteria. | | | |
| I know what I need to do to be successful. | | | |
| I don't give up when things get hard for me. | | | |
| I look for ways to grow in my learning. | | | |
| I have different strategies to use when I'm learning. | | | |
| I know what to do when I get stuck in my learning. | | | |
| I use feedback to help me understand my progress. | | | |
| I ask my classmates for feedback. | | | |
| I ask my teacher for feedback. | | | |
| I know that when I make mistakes, it helps me grow. | | | |
| I know when I have to make changes in my learning. | | | |
| I can use the learning intention and success criteria to monitor my progress. | | | |
| I know what I need to do next to grow in my learning. | | | |
| I learn from my classmates during my learning. | | | |
| I teach my classmates when they don't understand something. | | | |

**Time for Action**

Think about **one** of the areas where you checked "some of the time" or "none of the time." What is an action you can take to help further develop that area? Capture your action step below.

# Student Goal Setting Template

Date: _____

## Step 1: Identify the *what* and *why* of my goal.

What is my goal?

Why is this my goal?

## Is my goal SMARTER?

**S** | **Specific**
How is my goal specific?

**M** | **Measurable**
How is my goal measurable?

**A** | **Ambitious**
How is my goal ambitious?

**R** | **Results-oriented**
How is my goal results-oriented?

**T** | **Time bound**
How is my goal time bound?

**E** | **Evaluate**
How will I evaluate my goal?

**R** | **Reevaluate**
How will I reevaluate my plan to reach my goal?

## Step 2: Make an action plan and carry it out.

What is my plan for reaching my goal?

What resources do I have available to help me in reaching my goal?

How will I determine my progress toward reaching my goal?

When will I evaluate my goal and determine my next learning steps?

## Step 3: Reflect on, revise, and refine my goal.

What actions have I taken so far to support me in meeting my goal?

What evidence do I have to determine the impact of those action steps?

Does the evidence that I have show growth toward where I want to be?

Based on my evidence, do I need to make any adjustments or revisions to my goal? If so, what?

# Student Goal Setting Template

Date: _____

## Step 1: Identify the *what* and *why* of my goal.

What is my goal?

Why is this my goal?

## Is my goal SMARTER?

**S** | **Specific**
How is my goal specific?

**M** | **Measurable**
How is my goal measurable?

**A** | **Ambitious**
How is my goal ambitious?

**R** | **Results-oriented**
How is my goal results-oriented?

**T** | **Time bound**
How is my goal time bound?

**E** | **Evaluate**
How will I evaluate my goal?

**R** | **Reevaluate**
How will I reevaluate my plan to reach my goal?

## Step 2: Make an action plan and carry it out.

What is my plan for reaching my goal?

What resources do I have available to help me in reaching my goal?

How will I determine my progress toward reaching my goal?

When will I evaluate my goal and determine my next learning steps?

## Step 3: Reflect on, revise, and refine my goal.

What actions have I taken so far to support me in meeting my goal?

What evidence do I have to determine the impact of those action steps?

Does the evidence that I have show growth toward where I want to be?

Based on my evidence, do I need to make any adjustments or revisions to my goal? If so, what?

# Student Goal Setting Template

Date: _____

**Step 1: Identify the *what* and *why* of my goal.**

What is my goal?

Why is this my goal?

## Is my goal SMARTER?

**S** **Specific**
How is my goal specific?

**M** **Measurable**
How is my goal measurable?

**A** **Ambitious**
How is my goal ambitious?

**R** **Results-oriented**
How is my goal results-oriented?

**T** **Time bound**
How is my goal time bound?

**E** **Evaluate**
How will I evaluate my goal?

**R** **Reevaluate**
How will I reevaluate my plan to reach my goal?

## Step 2: Make an action plan and carry it out.

What is my plan for reaching my goal?

What resources do I have available to help me in reaching my goal?

How will I determine my progress toward reaching my goal?

When will I evaluate my goal and determine my next learning steps?

## Step 3: Reflect on, revise, and refine my goal.

What actions have I taken so far to support me in meeting my goal?

What evidence do I have to determine the impact of those action steps?

Does the evidence that I have show growth toward where I want to be?

Based on my evidence, do I need to make any adjustments or revisions to my goal? If so, what?

# Learning Intentions and Success Criteria Self-Assessment

Date: _____

| Part 1: What knowledge and experiences do you already have? | | | |
|---|---|---|---|
| **Skills and Concepts** | I have done this a lot before. | I have done this a little before. | This will be new for me. |
| **1** | | | |
| **2** | | | |
| **3** | | | |
| **4** | | | |

**Part 2**

What words or phrases are unclear?

What do I think they might mean?

**Turn and Talk**

Turn to a classmate and share what you captured in your self-assessment and why you checked the choices you did. Next, talk about any words and phrases that might be unclear and what you think they mean.

**Closing Reflection**

A critical part of becoming an assessment-capable visible learner is having a clear understanding of what the learning intentions and success criteria mean. What actions can you take on your own or with your classmates or teacher to ensure you understand the learning intentions of each lesson?

# Learning Intentions and Success Criteria Self-Assessment

Date: _____

| Part 1: What knowledge and experiences do you already have? | | | |
|---|---|---|---|
| **Skills and Concepts** | I have done this a lot before. | I have done this a little before. | This will be new for me. |
| **1** | | | |
| **2** | | | |
| **3** | | | |
| **4** | | | |

## Part 2

What words or phrases are unclear?

What do I think they might mean?

**Turn and Talk**

Turn to a classmate and share what you captured in your self-assessment and why you checked the choices you did. Next, talk about any words and phrases that might be unclear and what you think they mean.

**Closing Reflection**

A critical part of becoming an assessment-capable visible learner is having a clear understanding of what the learning intentions and success criteria mean. What actions can you take on your own or with your classmates or teacher to ensure you understand the learning intentions of each lesson?

# Learning Intentions and Success Criteria Self-Assessment

Date: _____

| Part 1: What knowledge and experiences do you already have? | | | |
|---|---|---|---|
| **Skills and Concepts** | I have done this a lot before. | I have done this a little before. | This will be new for me. |
| **1** | | | |
| **2** | | | |
| **3** | | | |
| **4** | | | |

**Part 2**

What words or phrases are unclear?

What do I think they might mean?

**Turn and Talk**

Turn to a classmate and share what you captured in your self-assessment and why you checked the choices you did. Next, talk about any words and phrases that might be unclear and what you think they mean.

**Closing Reflection**

A critical part of becoming an assessment-capable visible learner is having a clear understanding of what the learning intentions and success criteria mean. What actions can you take on your own or with your classmates or teacher to ensure you understand the learning intentions of each lesson?

# Co-constructing Success Criteria Template

**Date:** _____

| | |
|---|---|
| **Today's Learning Intention(s):** | |
| **Success Criteria:** | What would you need to be able to do as evidence that you mastered the learning intention(s)? |

Now that we've taken the time to co-construct success criteria for our learning intention(s), think about the following questions:

1. What will be something that is challenging for you?

2. What will be something you can easily do?

# Co-constructing Success Criteria Template

**Date:** _____

| | |
|---|---|
| **Today's Learning Intention(s):** | |
| **Success Criteria:** | What would you need to be able to do as evidence that you mastered the learning intention(s)? |

Now that we've taken the time to co-construct success criteria for our learning intention(s), think about the following questions:

1. What will be something that is challenging for you?


2. What will be something you can easily do?

# Co-constructing Success Criteria Template

**Date:** _____

| Today's Learning Intention(s): | |
|---|---|
| Success Criteria: | What would you need to be able to do as evidence that you mastered the learning intention(s)? |

Now that we've taken the time to co-construct success criteria for our learning intention(s), think about the following questions:

1. What will be something that is challenging for you?

2. What will be something you can easily do?

# Self-Assessing Your Progress Using Success Criteria Template

Date: _____

**Directions:** Capture the success criteria for the learning intention provided by your teacher in the boxes below. Prior to the end of the lesson, self-assess your progress by determining your performance level for each success criterion below.

|  | I'm a pro and can teach others. | I'm able to do this on my own. | I'm still practicing but almost there. | I need more help. |
|---|---|---|---|---|
| **SUCCESS CRITERIA 1:** |  |  |  |  |

Evidence to support current performance level:

My next learning steps:

| **SUCCESS CRITERIA 2:** |  |  |  |  |
|---|---|---|---|---|

Evidence to support current performance level:

My next learning steps:

| | I'm a pro and can teach others. | I'm able to do this on my own. | I'm still practicing but almost there. | I need more help. |
|---|---|---|---|---|
| **SUCCESS CRITERIA 3:** | | | | |

Evidence to support current performance level:

My next learning steps:

| | | | | |
|---|---|---|---|---|
| **SUCCESS CRITERIA 4:** | | | | |

Evidence to support current performance level:

My next learning steps:

# Self-Assessing Your Progress Using Success Criteria Template

**Date:** _____

**Directions:** Capture the success criteria for the learning intention provided by your teacher in the boxes below. Prior to the end of the lesson, self-assess your progress by determining your performance level for each success criterion below.

|  | I'm a pro and can teach others. | I'm able to do this on my own. | I'm still practicing but almost there. | I need more help. |
|---|---|---|---|---|
| **SUCCESS CRITERIA 1:** |  |  |  |  |

Evidence to support current performance level:

My next learning steps:

| **SUCCESS CRITERIA 2:** |  |  |  |  |
|---|---|---|---|---|

Evidence to support current performance level:

My next learning steps:

| | I'm a pro and can teach others. | I'm able to do this on my own. | I'm still practicing but almost there. | I need more help. |
|---|---|---|---|---|
| **SUCCESS CRITERIA 3:** | | | | |

Evidence to support current performance level:

My next learning steps:

| | | | | |
|---|---|---|---|---|
| **SUCCESS CRITERIA 4:** | | | | |

Evidence to support current performance level:

My next learning steps:

# Self-Assessing Your Progress Using Success Criteria Template

**Date:** _____

**Directions:** Capture the success criteria for the learning intention provided by your teacher in the boxes below. Prior to the end of the lesson, self-assess your progress by determining your performance level for each success criterion below.

|  | I'm a pro and can teach others. | I'm able to do this on my own. | I'm still practicing but almost there. | I need more help. |
|---|---|---|---|---|
| **SUCCESS CRITERIA 1:** |  |  |  |  |
| Evidence to support current performance level: |  |  |  |  |
| My next learning steps: |  |  |  |  |
| **SUCCESS CRITERIA 2:** |  |  |  |  |

Evidence to support current performance level:

My next learning steps:

| | I'm a pro and can teach others. | I'm able to do this on my own. | I'm still practicing but almost there. | I need more help. |
|---|---|---|---|---|
| **SUCCESS CRITERIA 3:** | | | | |

Evidence to support current performance level:

My next learning steps:

| | | | | |
|---|---|---|---|---|
| **SUCCESS CRITERIA 4:** | | | | |

Evidence to support current performance level:

My next learning steps:

# Learning Strategies Checklist

Date: _____

**Directions:** Think about what you are learning today. Check the boxes that most closely reflect your learning task.

## Today your task entails...

| | | |
|---|---|---|
| Writing an essay/paper | Solving problems | ☐ Analyzing ideas, concepts and/or characters |
| Reading an article | Giving a presentation | ☐ Creating a project |
| Studying a novel | Taking an assessment/ test/quiz | ☐ Evaluating ideas, concepts and/or characters |
| Conducting an experiment | Learning a new concept or idea | ☐ Writing a lab report |
| Working (collaboratively) in a group | Analyzing data | ☐ Developing a timeline |
| | | ☐ Other |

**Directions:** Look at the list of strategies below. Check at least one strategy that you will use to support you in what you are learning today.

## Learning Strategies

| | | |
|---|---|---|
| Note-taking | Annotating | ☐ Self-questioning |
| Outlining | Repeated reading | ☐ Self-monitoring |
| Graphic organizer | Summarizing | ☐ Planning for the task |
| Concept mapping | Organizing notes | ☐ Transforming information |
| Synthesizing information | Deconstructing information | ☐ Studying |

**Did it Work?**

Take a moment to think about the strategy you used in your learning today. Why did you select this strategy? Do you think that it supported you in your learning? Why or why not?

# Learning Strategies Checklist

Date: _____

**Directions:** Think about what you are learning today. Check the boxes that most closely reflect your learning task.

## Today your task entails...

| | | |
|---|---|---|
| Writing an essay/paper | Solving problems | ☐ Analyzing ideas, concepts and/or characters |
| Reading an article | Giving a presentation | ☐ Creating a project |
| Studying a novel | Taking an assessment/ test/quiz | ☐ Evaluating ideas, concepts and/or characters |
| Conducting an experiment | Learning a new concept or idea | ☐ Writing a lab report |
| Working (collaboratively) in a group | Analyzing data | ☐ Developing a timeline |
| | | ☐ Other |

**Directions:** Look at the list of strategies below. Check at least one strategy that you will use to support you in what you are learning today.

## Learning Strategies

| | | |
|---|---|---|
| Note-taking | Annotating | ☐ Self-questioning |
| Outlining | Repeated reading | ☐ Self-monitoring |
| Graphic organizer | Summarizing | ☐ Planning for the task |
| Concept mapping | Organizing notes | ☐ Transforming information |
| Synthesizing information | Deconstructing information | ☐ Studying |

Take a moment to think about the strategy you used in your learning today. Why did you select this strategy? Do you think that it supported you in your learning? Why or why not?

# Learning Strategies Checklist

Date: _____

**Directions:** Think about what you are learning today. Check the boxes that most closely reflect your learning task.

## Today your task entails...

| | | |
|---|---|---|
| Writing an essay/paper | ☐ Solving problems | ☐ Analyzing ideas, concepts and/or characters |
| Reading an article | ☐ Giving a presentation | ☐ Creating a project |
| Studying a novel | ☐ Taking an assessment/ test/quiz | ☐ Evaluating ideas, concepts and/or characters |
| Conducting an experiment | ☐ Learning a new concept or idea | ☐ Writing a lab report |
| Working (collaboratively) in a group | ☐ Analyzing data | ☐ Developing a timeline |
| | | ☐ Other |

**Directions:** Look at the list of strategies below. Check at least one strategy that you will use to support you in what you are learning today.

## Learning Strategies

| | | |
|---|---|---|
| Note-taking | Annotating | ☐ Self-questioning |
| Outlining | Repeated reading | ☐ Self-monitoring |
| Graphic organizer | Summarizing | ☐ Planning for the task |
| Concept mapping | Organizing notes | ☐ Transforming information |
| Synthesizing information | Deconstructing information | ☐ Studying |

**Did it Work?**

Take a moment to think about the strategy you used in your learning today. Why did you select this strategy? Do you think that it supported you in your learning? Why or why not?

# Study Skills Checklist

Date: _____

| Our learning intention: |
| I need practice with: |

Check the study skills below that you will use as part of your practice moving forward.

| Cognitive Study Skills | Metacognitive Study Skills | Affective Study Skills |
| --- | --- | --- |
| I can take notes. | I can plan for my task. | I can get motivated to study or practice. |
| I can use a graphic organizer. | I can monitor my learning. | I can structure my learning environment. |
| I can summarize. | I can review corrected work. | I can manage my time. |
| I can create flashcards. | I can revise my work. | I can manage my stress and anxiety. |
| I can use mnemonics. | I can self-assess. | I can set goals. |
| I can memorize important information. | I can use self-questioning. | I have a willingness to solve problems. |
| I can reread. | I can self-verbalize. | I desire to influence my own learning. |

# Study Skills Checklist

Date: _____

| Our learning intention: | |
| I need practice with: | |

Check the study skills below that you will use as part of your practice moving forward.

| Cognitive Study Skills | Metacognitive Study Skills | Affective Study Skills |
|---|---|---|
| I can take notes. | I can plan for my task. | ☐ I can get motivated to study or practice. |
| I can use a graphic organizer. | I can monitor my learning. | ☐ I can structure my learning environment. |
| I can summarize. | I can review corrected work. | ☐ I can manage my time. |
| I can create flashcards. | I can revise my work. | ☐ I can manage my stress and anxiety. |
| I can use mnemonics. | I can self-assess. | ☐ I can set goals. |
| I can memorize important information. | I can use self-questioning. | ☐ I have a willingness to solve problems. |
| I can reread. | I can self-verbalize. | ☐ I desire to influence my own learning. |

# Study Skills Checklist

Date: _____

| | |
|---|---|
| Our learning intention: | |
| I need practice with: | |

Check the study skills below that you will use as part of your practice moving forward.

| Cognitive Study Skills | Metacognitive Study Skills | Affective Study Skills |
|---|---|---|
| I can take notes. | I can plan for my task. | ☐ I can get motivated to study or practice. |
| I can use a graphic organizer. | I can monitor my learning. | ☐ I can structure my learning environment. |
| I can summarize. | I can review corrected work. | ☐ I can manage my time. |
| I can create flashcards. | I can revise my work. | ☐ I can manage my stress and anxiety. |
| I can use mnemonics. | I can self-assess. | ☐ I can set goals. |
| I can memorize important information. | I can use self-questioning. | ☐ I have a willingness to solve problems. |
| I can reread. | I can self-verbalize. | ☐ I desire to influence my own learning. |

# Is It Time for Feedback? Checklist

Date: _____

| | **I Can't Get Started in My Learning** | |
|---|---|---|
| **What can I do on my own?** | ☐ I reread the directions to make sure I didn't miss something. ☐ I reviewed the success criteria. ☐ I reviewed any examples and/or resources provided for my task. ☐ I looked online for examples of others' work. | |
| **What can I do with a peer?** | ☐ I asked my peer to clarify the task. ☐ I asked my peer to walk me through the question and/or problem. ☐ I asked my peer how they knew how to get started. ☐ I asked my peer to support me in getting the task started. | |
| **What can I do with the teacher?** | ☐ I clarified what the task is asking for. ☐ I walked through an example/exemplar with the teacher. ☐ I asked the teacher to support me in getting the task started. | |

| | **I Got Started, but I'm Not Sure Where to Go Next in My Learning** | |
|---|---|---|
| **What can I do on my own?** | ☐ I reviewed the success criteria. ☐ I reviewed any examples and/or resources provided for my task. ☐ I tried to determine where I need to go next based off of what I got started. ☐ I determined what I got right so far and why. | |
| **What can I do with a peer?** | ☐ I clarified what the task was asking for. ☐ I showed my work to my peer and asked for help in identifying my next step. ☐ I asked my peer to ask me questions about what I got started on my task. ☐ I asked my peer what they felt I had gotten right so far and why. | |
| **What can I do with the teacher?** | ☐ I clarified what the task is asking for. ☐ I asked for support in identifying my next step. ☐ I asked the teacher to model the portion of the task I misunderstand. | |

## I'm Finished with My Learning

| | |
|---|---|
| **What can I do on my own?** | I self-assessed my work against the success criteria.<br><br>I reviewed my work against the exemplar, if applicable.<br><br>I identified where I have strengths in my work to get even stronger.<br><br>I identified opportunities in my work to determine what my next learning step is. |
| **What can I do with a peer?** | I asked my peer if they agree that I met the success criteria.<br><br>I asked my peer to identify a strength in my work.<br><br>I asked my peer to identify an opportunity in my work. |
| **What can I do with the teacher?** | I asked my teacher if they agree that I met the success criteria.<br><br>I asked the teacher to identify a strength in my current work.<br><br>I asked the teacher to identify an opportunity in my current work. |

# Is It Time for Feedback? Checklist

Date: _____

| | I Can't Get Started in My Learning |
|---|---|
| **What can I do on my own?** | ☐ I reread the directions to make sure I didn't miss something.<br>☐ I reviewed the success criteria.<br>☐ I reviewed any examples and/or resources provided for my task.<br>☐ I looked online for examples of others' work. |
| **What can I do with a peer?** | ☐ I asked my peer to clarify the task.<br>☐ I asked my peer to walk me through the question and/or problem.<br>☐ I asked my peer how they knew how to get started.<br>☐ I asked my peer to support me in getting the task started. |
| **What can I do with the teacher?** | ☐ I clarified what the task is asking for.<br>☐ I walked through an example/exemplar with the teacher.<br>☐ I asked the teacher to support me in getting the task started. |

| | I Got Started, but I'm Not Sure Where to Go Next in My Learning |
|---|---|
| **What can I do on my own?** | ☐ I reviewed the success criteria.<br>☐ I reviewed any examples and/or resources provided for my task.<br>☐ I tried to determine where I need to go next based off of what I got started.<br>☐ I determined what I got right so far and why. |
| **What can I do with a peer?** | ☐ I clarified what the task was asking for.<br>☐ I showed my work to my peer and asked for help in identifying my next step.<br>☐ I asked my peer to ask me questions about what I got started on my task.<br>☐ I asked my peer what they felt I had gotten right so far and why. |
| **What can I do with the teacher?** | ☐ I clarified what the task is asking for.<br>☐ I asked for support in identifying my next step.<br>☐ I asked the teacher to model the portion of the task I misunderstand. |

| | I'm Finished with My Learning |
|---|---|
| **What can I do on my own?** | I self-assessed my work against the success criteria.<br><br>I reviewed my work against the exemplar, if applicable.<br><br>I identified where I have strengths in my work to get even stronger.<br><br>I identified opportunities in my work to determine what my next learning step is. |
| **What can I do with a peer?** | I asked my peer if they agree that I met the success criteria.<br><br>I asked my peer to identify a strength in my work.<br><br>I asked my peer to identify an opportunity in my work. |
| **What can I do with the teacher?** | I asked my teacher if they agree that I met the success criteria.<br><br>I asked the teacher to identify a strength in my current work.<br><br>I asked the teacher to identify an opportunity in my current work. |

# Is It Time for Feedback? Checklist

Date: _____

| **I Can't Get Started in My Learning** | |
|---|---|
| **What can I do on my own?** | ☐ I reread the directions to make sure I didn't miss something.<br>☐ I reviewed the success criteria.<br>☐ I reviewed any examples and/or resources provided for my task.<br>☐ I looked online for examples of others' work. |
| **What can I do with a peer?** | ☐ I asked my peer to clarify the task.<br>☐ I asked my peer to walk me through the question and/or problem.<br>☐ I asked my peer how they knew how to get started.<br>☐ I asked my peer to support me in getting the task started. |
| **What can I do with the teacher?** | ☐ I clarified what the task is asking for.<br>☐ I walked through an example/exemplar with the teacher.<br>☐ I asked the teacher to support me in getting the task started. |

| **I Got Started, but I'm Not Sure Where to Go Next in My Learning** | |
|---|---|
| **What can I do on my own?** | ☐ I reviewed the success criteria.<br>☐ I reviewed any examples and/or resources provided for my task.<br>☐ I tried to determine where I need to go next based off of what I got started.<br>☐ I determined what I got right so far and why. |
| **What can I do with a peer?** | ☐ I clarified what the task was asking for.<br>☐ I showed my work to my peer and asked for help in identifying my next step.<br>☐ I asked my peer to ask me questions about what I got started on my task.<br>☐ I asked my peer what they felt I had gotten right so far and why. |
| **What can I do with the teacher?** | ☐ I clarified what the task is asking for.<br>☐ I asked for support in identifying my next step.<br>☐ I asked the teacher to model the portion of the task I misunderstand. |

## I'm Finished with My Learning

| | |
|---|---|
| **What can I do on my own?** | I self-assessed my work against the success criteria.<br><br>I reviewed my work against the exemplar, if applicable.<br><br>I identified where I have strengths in my work to get even stronger.<br><br>I identified opportunities in my work to determine what my next learning step is. |
| **What can I do with a peer?** | I asked my peer if they agree that I met the success criteria.<br><br>I asked my peer to identify a strength in my work.<br><br>I asked my peer to identify an opportunity in my work. |
| **What can I do with the teacher?** | I asked my teacher if they agree that I met the success criteria.<br><br>I asked the teacher to identify a strength in my current work.<br><br>I asked the teacher to identify an opportunity in my current work. |

Date:

**Feedback Question Card**

| FIRST | **Think about...** |
|---|---|

- Am I stuck? If so, where?
- Do I understand the success criteria?
- What have I gotten right so far?
- Where am I missing something?
- Am I close?
- Are the strategies I am using working? How do I know?

**NEXT** **Identify your feedback question(s) and capture it below...**

---
✂ - - - - - - - - - - - - - - - - - - - - - - - - - - - - - - - - - - - - - - - - - - - - - - - - - - - - - - - - - - - -
---

Date:

**Feedback Question Card**

| FIRST | **Think about...** |
|---|---|

- Am I stuck? If so, where?
- Do I understand the success criteria?
- What have I gotten right so far?
- Where am I missing something?
- Am I close?
- Are the strategies I am using working? How do I know?

**NEXT** **Identify your feedback question(s) and capture it below...**

**Date:**

**Feedback Question Card**

| FIRST | Think about... |
|---|---|

- Am I stuck? If so, where?
- Do I understand the success criteria?
- What have I gotten right so far?
- Where am I missing something?
- Am I close?
- Are the strategies I am using working? How do I know?

| NEXT | Identify your feedback question(s) and capture it below... |
|---|---|

**Date:**

**Feedback Question Card**

| FIRST | Think about... |
|---|---|

- Am I stuck? If so, where?
- Do I understand the success criteria?
- What have I gotten right so far?
- Where am I missing something?
- Am I close?
- Are the strategies I am using working? How do I know?

| NEXT | Identify your feedback question(s) and capture it below... |
|---|---|

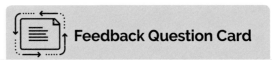
**Feedback Question Card**

**Date:**

FIRST  **Think about...**

- Am I stuck? If so, where?
- Do I understand the success criteria?
- What have I gotten right so far?
- Where am I missing something?
- Am I close?
- Are the strategies I am using working? How do I know?

NEXT  **Identify your feedback question(s) and capture it below...**

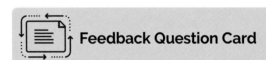
**Feedback Question Card**

**Date:**

FIRST  **Think about...**

- Am I stuck? If so, where?
- Do I understand the success criteria?
- What have I gotten right so far?
- Where am I missing something?
- Am I close?
- Are the strategies I am using working? How do I know?

NEXT  **Identify your feedback question(s) and capture it below...**

**Date:**

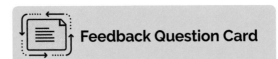

**FIRST** Think about...

- Am I stuck? If so, where?
- Do I understand the success criteria?
- What have I gotten right so far?
- Where am I missing something?
- Am I close?
- Are the strategies I am using working? How do I know?

**NEXT** Identify your feedback question(s) and capture it below...

---

**Date:**

**Feedback Question Card**

**FIRST** Think about...

- Am I stuck? If so, where?
- Do I understand the success criteria?
- What have I gotten right so far?
- Where am I missing something?
- Am I close?
- Are the strategies I am using working? How do I know?

**NEXT** Identify your feedback question(s) and capture it below...

Date:

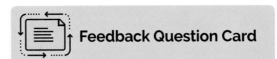

**Feedback Question Card**

**FIRST** Think about...

- Am I stuck? If so, where?
- Do I understand the success criteria?
- What have I gotten right so far?
- Where am I missing something?
- Am I close?
- Are the strategies I am using working? How do I know?

**NEXT** Identify your feedback question(s) and capture it below...

---

Date:

**Feedback Question Card**

**FIRST** Think about...

- Am I stuck? If so, where?
- Do I understand the success criteria?
- What have I gotten right so far?
- Where am I missing something?
- Am I close?
- Are the strategies I am using working? How do I know?

**NEXT** Identify your feedback question(s) and capture it below...

Date:

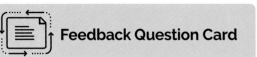

**Feedback Question Card**

| FIRST | Think about... |

- Am I stuck? If so, where?
- Do I understand the success criteria?
- What have I gotten right so far?
- Where am I missing something?
- Am I close?
- Are the strategies I am using working? How do I know?

| NEXT | Identify your feedback question(s) and capture it below... |

Date:

**Feedback Question Card**

| FIRST | Think about... |

- Am I stuck? If so, where?
- Do I understand the success criteria?
- What have I gotten right so far?
- Where am I missing something?
- Am I close?
- Are the strategies I am using working? How do I know?

| NEXT | Identify your feedback question(s) and capture it below... |

# Reflecting on Errors as Opportunities to Learn Template

Date: _____

**Directions:** Read and review the questions on your assessment. As you go through each one, place the question number in one of the four quadrants below.

Questions that I thought were
**EASY** that I got **WRONG**

Questions that I thought were
**HARD** that I got **WRONG**

Questions that I thought were
**EASY** that I got **RIGHT**

Questions that I thought were
**HARD** that I got **RIGHT**

## Questions that I thought were **EASY** that I got **WRONG**.

| Question #: | Why did you get it wrong? |
| --- | --- |
| | What do you need to learn to get it right next time? |

| Question #: | Why did you get it wrong? |
| --- | --- |
| | What do you need to learn to get it right next time? |

| Question #: | Why did you get it wrong? |
| --- | --- |
| | What do you need to learn to get it right next time? |

| Question #: | Why did you get it wrong? |
| --- | --- |
| | What do you need to learn to get it right next time? |

## Questions that I thought were **HARD** that I got **WRONG**.

**Question #:**

What about the question was hard for you?

What do you need to learn to get it right next time?

**Question #:**

What about the question was hard for you?

What do you need to learn to get it right next time?

**Question #:**

What about the question was hard for you?

What do you need to learn to get it right next time?

**Question #:**

What about the question was hard for you?

What do you need to learn to get it right next time?

# Reflecting on Errors as Opportunities to Learn Template

**Date:** _____

**Directions:** Read and review the questions on your assessment. As you go through each one, place the question number in one of the four quadrants below.

Questions that I thought were
**EASY** that I got **WRONG**

Questions that I thought were
**HARD** that I got **WRONG**

Questions that I thought were
**EASY** that I got **RIGHT**

Questions that I thought were
**HARD** that I got **RIGHT**

## Questions that I thought were **EASY** that I got **WRONG**.

**Question #:**

Why did you get it wrong?

What do you need to learn to get it right next time?

**Question #:**

Why did you get it wrong?

What do you need to learn to get it right next time?

**Question #:**

Why did you get it wrong?

What do you need to learn to get it right next time?

**Question #:**

Why did you get it wrong?

What do you need to learn to get it right next time?

## Questions that I thought were **HARD** that I got **WRONG**.

| Question #: | What about the question was hard for you? |
| | |
| | What do you need to learn to get it right next time? |

| Question #: | What about the question was hard for you? |
| | |
| | What do you need to learn to get it right next time? |

| Question #: | What about the question was hard for you? |
| | |
| | What do you need to learn to get it right next time? |

| Question #: | What about the question was hard for you? |
| | |
| | What do you need to learn to get it right next time? |

# Reflecting on Errors as Opportunities to Learn Template

Date: _____

**Directions:** Read and review the questions on your assessment. As you go through each one, place the question number in one of the four quadrants below.

Questions that I thought were
**EASY** that I got **WRONG**

Questions that I thought were
**HARD** that I got **WRONG**

Questions that I thought were
**EASY** that I got **RIGHT**

Questions that I thought were
**HARD** that I got **RIGHT**

## Questions that I thought were **EASY** that I got **WRONG**.

| Question #: | Why did you get it wrong? |
| --- | --- |
| | |
| | What do you need to learn to get it right next time? |

| Question #: | Why did you get it wrong? |
| --- | --- |
| | |
| | What do you need to learn to get it right next time? |

| Question #: | Why did you get it wrong? |
| --- | --- |
| | |
| | What do you need to learn to get it right next time? |

| Question #: | Why did you get it wrong? |
| --- | --- |
| | |
| | What do you need to learn to get it right next time? |

## Questions that I thought were **HARD** that I got **WRONG**.

**Question #:**

What about the question was hard for you?

What do you need to learn to get it right next time?

**Question #:**

What about the question was hard for you?

What do you need to learn to get it right next time?

**Question #:**

What about the question was hard for you?

What do you need to learn to get it right next time?

**Question #:**

What about the question was hard for you?

What do you need to learn to get it right next time?

# Using Self-Questioning to Guide Your Learning Template

**Date:** _____

Self-questioning is when you generate questions to ask yourself during different phases of your learning. Asking yourself questions *before, during*, and *after* you engage in learning tasks is a strategy you can use to help yourself develop as an assessment-capable visible learner. Today, we will practice applying self-questioning to the lesson we are going to focus on.

## BEFORE THE LESSON...

What am I learning today? What is the learning intention?

What do I already know about this?

What do I want to know about this?

What do I need to do or find out?

**DURING THE LESSON...**

What am I finding out?

What questions do I have as I'm learning?

What is confusing to me?

What do I still need to find out?

**AFTER THE LESSON...**

What did I learn as a result of the lesson?

What is still confusing or challenging for me?

What do I still need to do moving forward?

# Using Self-Questioning to Guide Your Learning Template

**Date:** _____

Self-questioning is when you generate questions to ask yourself during different phases of your learning. Asking yourself questions *before, during*, and *after* you engage in learning tasks is a strategy you can use to help yourself develop as an assessment-capable visible learner. Today, we will practice applying self-questioning to the lesson we are going to focus on.

## BEFORE THE LESSON...

What am I learning today? What is the learning intention?

What do I already know about this?

What do I want to know about this?

What do I need to do or find out?

**DURING THE LESSON...**

What am I finding out?

What questions do I have as I'm learning?

What is confusing to me?

What do I still need to find out?

**AFTER THE LESSON...**

What did I learn as a result of the lesson?

What is still confusing or challenging for me?

What do I still need to do moving forward?

# Using Self-Questioning to Guide Your Learning Template

**Date:** _____

Self-questioning is when you generate questions to ask yourself during different phases of your learning. Asking yourself questions *before, during,* and *after* you engage in learning tasks is a strategy you can use to help yourself develop as an assessment-capable visible learner. Today, we will practice applying self-questioning to the lesson we are going to focus on.

## BEFORE THE LESSON...

What am I learning today? What is the learning intention?

What do I already know about this?

What do I want to know about this?

What do I need to do or find out?

**DURING THE LESSON...**

What am I finding out?

What questions do I have as I'm learning?

What is confusing to me?

What do I still need to find out?

**AFTER THE LESSON...**

What did I learn as a result of the lesson?

What is still confusing or challenging for me?

What do I still need to do moving forward?

# Checklist for Peer Teaching with Think-Alouds

**Date:** _____

## Thinking during a Think-Aloud Checklist

Let everyone who will be listening to your think-aloud read through the question or text before you begin your think-aloud.

Use "I" statements.

Share what you are reading about.

Talk about what is catching your attention as a reader.

Explain why you think you are correct using evidence in the text.

Don't go too fast or too slow.

Determine any actions you are taking as a result of what you are thinking about as you read.

Share why you are taking the actions you are taking.

Make sure your think-aloud isn't longer than five minutes.

1. What was it like *doing* a think-aloud for your peer(s)? Did it support you in what you were learning today? Why or why not?

2. What was it like *listening* to a think-aloud from your peer(s)? Did it support you in what you were learning today? Why or why not?

# Checklist for Peer Teaching with Think-Alouds

**Date:** _____

Let everyone who will be listening to your think-aloud read through the question or text before you begin your think-aloud.

Use "I" statements.

Share what you are reading about.

Talk about what is catching your attention as a reader.

Explain why you think you are correct using evidence in the text.

Don't go too fast or too slow.

Determine any actions you are taking as a result of what you are thinking about as you read.

Share why you are taking the actions you are taking.

Make sure your think-aloud isn't longer than five minutes.

**Stop & Reflect**

1. What was it like *doing* a think-aloud for your peer(s)? Did it support you in what you were learning today? Why or why not?

2. What was it like *listening* to a think-aloud from your peer(s)? Did it support you in what you were learning today? Why or why not?

# Checklist for Peer Teaching with Think-Alouds

**Date:** _____

| Thinking during a Think-Aloud Checklist |
|---|

Let everyone who will be listening to your think-aloud read through the question or text before you begin your think-aloud.

Use "I" statements.

Share what you are reading about.

Talk about what is catching your attention as a reader.

Explain why you think you are correct using evidence in the text.

Don't go too fast or too slow.

Determine any actions you are taking as a result of what you are thinking about as you read.

Share why you are taking the actions you are taking.

Make sure your think-aloud isn't longer than five minutes.

**Stop & Reflect**

1. What was it like *doing* a think-aloud for your peer(s)? Did it support you in what you were learning today? Why or why not?

2. What was it like *listening* to a think-aloud from your peer(s)? Did it support you in what you were learning today? Why or why not?

# Student Sentence Starters for Reciprocal Teaching

Date: _____

| | |
|---|---|
| **Summarizing** | • Key details in this passage are... <br><br> • Key information included in this passage is... <br><br> • The main idea/message of the passage is... <br><br> • A theme I can see is... <br><br> • A summary of what we just read is... |
| **Questioning** | • What does the passage mean where it said...? <br><br> • Why did the author choose to include...? (This could be key vocabulary, pictures, symbols, graphs, etc.) <br><br> • What is the point of...? <br><br> • Why is ... happening? <br><br> • What is the relationship between...? (This could be relationships between characters, ideas, concepts, numbers, places, etc.) <br><br> • What can we infer about...? (This could be relationships between characters, ideas, concepts, numbers, places, etc.) <br><br> • What evidence in the text supports...? |
| **Clarifying** | • Is the author saying... about...? <br><br> • What does this word or phrase mean? (Share the word or phrase with the group.) <br><br> • Can you elaborate on what you just said about...? <br><br> • Tell me more about...? <br><br> • What evidence supports what you just shared? <br><br> • Can you give me an example of...? |
| **Predicting** | • I think the next passage we read is going to be about... <br><br> • Information that will probably be a part of the next passage is... <br><br> • I bet we'll learn more about...in the next passage. <br><br> • I think we'll find out about...in the next passage. |

# Student Sentence Starters for Reciprocal Teaching

**Date:** _____

| | |
|---|---|
| **Summarizing** | • Key details in this passage are…<br><br>• Key information included in this passage is…<br><br>• The main idea/message of the passage is…<br><br>• A theme I can see is…<br><br>• A summary of what we just read is… |
| **Questioning** | • What does the passage mean where it said…?<br><br>• Why did the author choose to include…? (This could be key vocabulary, pictures, symbols, graphs, etc.)<br><br>• What is the point of…?<br><br>• Why is … happening?<br><br>• What is the relationship between…? (This could be relationships between characters, ideas, concepts, numbers, places, etc.)<br><br>• What can we infer about…? (This could be relationships between characters, ideas, concepts, numbers, places, etc.)<br><br>• What evidence in the text supports…? |
| **Clarifying** | • Is the author saying… about…?<br><br>• What does this word or phrase mean? (Share the word or phrase with the group.)<br><br>• Can you elaborate on what you just said about…?<br><br>• Tell me more about…?<br><br>• What evidence supports what you just shared?<br><br>• Can you give me an example of…? |
| **Predicting** | • I think the next passage we read is going to be about…<br><br>• Information that will probably be a part of the next passage is…<br><br>• I bet we'll learn more about…in the next passage.<br><br>• I think we'll find out about…in the next passage. |

# Student Sentence Starters for Reciprocal Teaching

Date: _____

| | |
|---|---|
| **Summarizing** | • Key details in this passage are... <br><br> • Key information included in this passage is... <br><br> • The main idea/message of the passage is... <br><br> • A theme I can see is... <br><br> • A summary of what we just read is... |
| **Questioning** | • What does the passage mean where it said...? <br><br> • Why did the author choose to include...? (This could be key vocabulary, pictures, symbols, graphs, etc.) <br><br> • What is the point of...? <br><br> • Why is ... happening? <br><br> • What is the relationship between...? (This could be relationships between characters, ideas, concepts, numbers, places, etc.) <br><br> • What can we infer about...? (This could be relationships between characters, ideas, concepts, numbers, places, etc.) <br><br> • What evidence in the text supports...? |
| **Clarifying** | • Is the author saying... about...? <br><br> • What does this word or phrase mean? (Share the word or phrase with the group.) <br><br> • Can you elaborate on what you just said about...? <br><br> • Tell me more about...? <br><br> • What evidence supports what you just shared? <br><br> • Can you give me an example of...? |
| **Predicting** | • I think the next passage we read is going to be about... <br><br> • Information that will probably be a part of the next passage is... <br><br> • I bet we'll learn more about...in the next passage. <br><br> • I think we'll find out about...in the next passage. |

A SAGE Publishing Company

**CORWIN HAS ONE MISSION:** to enhance education through intentional professional learning.

We build long-term relationships with our authors, educators, clients, and associations who partner with us to develop and continuously improve the best evidence-based practices that establish and support lifelong learning.